ASTROLOGY
in the **WORKPLACE**

ASTROLOGY in the WORKPLACE

The Zodiac Guide to Creating Great Working Relationships

Penny Thornton

ARCTURUS

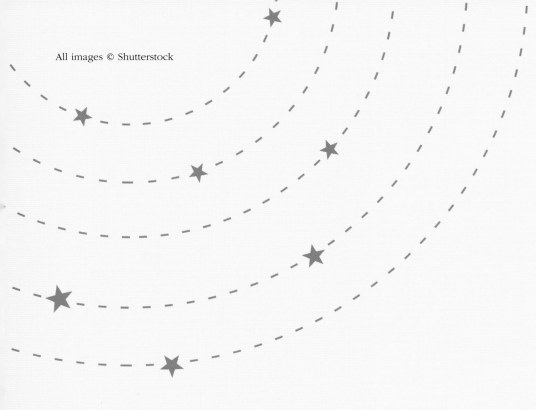

ARCTURUS

This edition published in 2019 by Arcturus Publishing Limited
26/27 Bickels Yard, 151–153 Bermondsey Street,
London SE1 3HA

ISBN: 978-1-78828-048-8
AD005922UK

Printed in China

CONTENTS

Introduction: How Astrology Works   8

THE FIRE SIGNS   17

The element fire   18
Fire on a scale of 1–10   22

Aries in the workplace   24
  Curriculum vitae   24
  The Aries boss   26
  The Aries employee   29

Leo in the workplace   34
  Curriculum vitae   34
  The Leo boss   37
  The Leo employee   40

Sagittarius in the workplace   44
  Curriculum vitae   44
  The Sagittarian boss   47
  The Sagittarian employee   50

Inter-relationships   54

THE EARTH SIGNS   61

The element earth   62
Earth on a scale of 1–10   66

Taurus in the workplace   68
Curriculum vitae   68
The Taurus boss   71
The Taurus employee   74

Virgo in the workplace   78
Curriculum vitae   78
The Virgo boss   80
The Virgo employee   84

Capricorn in the workplace   88
Curriculum vitae   88
The Capricorn boss   90
The Capricorn employee   94

Inter-relationships   98

THE AIR SIGNS   105

The element air   106
Air on a scale of 1–10   109

Gemini in the workplace   112
Curriculum vitae   112
The Gemini boss   115
The Gemini employee   117

Libra in the workplace   122
Curriculum vitae   122
The Libran boss   124
The Libra employee   127

Aquarius in the workplace   **132**
    Curriculum vitae   132
    The Aquarius boss   134
    The Aquarius employee   137

Inter-relationships   **142**

THE WATER SIGNS   149

The element water   **150**
    Water on a scale of 1–10   154

Cancer in the workplace   **156**
    Curriculum vitae   156
    The Cancer boss   158
    The Cancer employee   161

Scorpio in the workplace   **166**
    Curriculum vitae   166
    The Scorpio boss   168
    The Scorpio employee   171

Pisces in the workplace   **176**
    Curriculum vitae   176
    The Pisces boss   178
    The Pisces employee   181

Inter-relationships   **186**

Acknowledgements   **192**

INTRODUCTION
HOW ASTROLOGY WORKS

To the elements it came from,
Everything will return.
Our bodies to earth,
Our blood to water,
Heat to fire,
Breath to air.
Empedocles on Etna, by Matthew Arnold

I boldly called this introduction 'How Astrology Works', but I have no idea how astrology works. No one has. We have *theories*, of course – and I will be covering them shortly – but thus far no one has put forward a scientifically provable mechanism to explain it. Which is why, in 1975, 186 astronomers, physicists and leading scientists felt compelled to sign a statement denouncing astrology. Opinions have not changed.

Now, before you decide this book has no merit whatsoever, hold the phone. In accountancy there is a term known as QBE – Qualified By Experience – which applies to an accountant who is qualified to perform the functions of the job on an equal footing with those who have formal professional membership. You see where I'm going. Astrology's proof lies in its long, long practice. It is qualified by experience. It began thousands of years ago and its ancient principles are still as valid today as they were back in 2,500 BCE.

The earliest evidence that humans were aware of and interested in the stars and the heavens comes from the Aurignacian Culture of Europe (c. 32,000 BCE) in the form of markings on animal bones clearly depicting the lunar phases. Tablets containing astrological texts from the third millennia BCE display a similar preoccupation with the movements of the planets and the constellations, and by the time of Plato (427–347 BCE) and Ptolemy (c. 100–170 CE) astrology was flourishing. It was the province of the learned of their day, and was no doubt the method by which the magi arrived in Bethlehem to pay their respects to the newborn king. The star they followed, incidentally, was almost certainly the great Jupiter–Saturn triple conjunction in Pisces of 7 CE[1].

Astrology lost its standing in the 17th century when the advance of science led to a greater understanding of the solar system and the universe beyond. The science of astronomy was born, forcing astrology, with its geocentric view of the universe, underground. And it remained underground for 200 years when it was reborn thanks to the spiritualism movement and the advent of depth psychology.

I began my astrological studies at the peak of its renaissance in the late 1970s. Joining the Faculty of Astrological Studies and the Astrological Association of Great Britain I attended lectures given at the National Liberal Club by newcomers Liz Greene and Howard Sasportas and such legends as John Addey and Dennis Elwell. There was standing room only at those lectures and some of us would gather in the pub around the corner afterwards and talk eclipses, 7th harmonic principles and unaspected Saturns until the bell sounded for 'last orders'. It was a heady period and out of it came new understandings.

The pioneering work of Swiss psychiatrist and founder of analytical psychology, Carl Jung, concerning dreams, archetypal images and astrological themes as well as his theory of synchronicity gave astrologers not only greater insight into the subject but also a potential mechanism for how astrology worked. Of which we will hear more later.

At the same time, as a more psychologically based astrology was developing, taking it far away from its prediction-oriented roots, strides were being made on the scientific side of things. The Journal of Research in Astrology, *Correlation* published its first edition in 1981 and has since covered every significant study in astrology over the past 37 years. Still no proof, though.

For a long while, my interest was focused on proving astrology, but as time went by the practice of astrology became more important than the theory. Day after day in my consulting rooms I saw astrology working in people's lives. I watched events on the world's stage unfold with the requisite astrological signatures. My ability to interpret a chart depended not on any psychic promptings – I saw no events appear as if on a screen before my eyes; no unseen figure whispered in my ear. I simply

---

1   This triple conjunction of the then two outermost planets of the solar system in the mystical sign of Pisces – an event so rare it only takes place every 900 years – was a portent of the arrival of a great king.

used the techniques I had learned over the years – techniques handed down from generation to generation of astrologers – to make informed judgements.

If astrology suffered a hammer blow in the 17th century, when it became separated from the emerging science of astronomy, it suffered a second blow in the 1930s with the advent of sun-sign astrology.

In 1930 the editor of the *Sunday Express* asked leading astrologer, Richard Naylor, to interpret the horoscope of the newly born Princess Margaret. At the end of the article, which proved immensely popular, Naylor wrote predictions for the 12 signs of the zodiac based on each sun sign. And so pop-astrology was born.

From the outset the serious astrological faction believed sun-sign astrology trivialized the subject, and for the last 90 years has fiercely opposed it and treated those astrologers who write star columns with contempt. I, however, take a different view. And it's a good job because otherwise *Astrology in the Workplace* would never have been written!

In 1986, an article in the *Daily Mail* about my book *Romancing the Stars*, in which I had suggested Prince Charles might never be king, led to offers from magazines in Norway and Britain to write a sun-sign column. And being a pioneering, fearless Aries, I took up the challenge. In 1992 that challenge became even more acute when I took on a daily sun-sign forecast in *Today* newspaper.

Far from compromising my technical skills, writing a daily column sharpened them. I was constantly monitoring the movements of the planets and observing their signatures on national and international events and on the lives of ordinary people and celebrities. And by examining the forthcoming alignments through the lenses of the 12 sun signs I was able to make general forecasts. I still do.

A sun sign, of course, is only part of a far more complex picture. In a natal chart, the sun, the moon and the eight planets, the angles between them all, plus the rising sign (the Ascendant) and the culminating sign (the Mid-heaven) are taken into consideration, which makes for a much more accurate and detailed interpretation.

Nonetheless, the sign the sun is in at birth has a big part to play in who we are and how we behave.

I compare the sun sign to a nationality. We all have an opinion of, say, the Italians or the French or the way the Brits or the Aussies tend to behave; likewise, we notice similarities in all Leos and all Scorpios and so on. In this way I have been able to provide broad behavioural trends in the 12 signs of the zodiac in reference to their roles as bosses and employees in the workplace.

In order to fulfil the task of bringing zodiac life into the workplace, I divided the 12 signs into four groups according to their element – fire, earth, air and water. And there is another important and relevant subdivision which I have used – the *modalities* – which breaks the 12 zodiac signs into groups of three – Cardinal, Fixed or Mutable. In this way each sign of the zodiac is a unique combination of an element and a modality.

Fourfold divisions form part of most metaphysical systems. In the Middle Ages you'd be treated for your medical problems according to your temperament – choleric (fire), melancholic (earth), sanguine (air) and phlegmatic (water). There are four fundamental states of matter in modern physics – solid (earth), liquid (water), gas (air) and plasma (fire). From a spiritual perspective the elements represent

lessons the soul must learn to evolve – fiery people must learn to love, earthy people to serve; for air the lesson is brotherhood and for water peace. And most relevant to astrology are Jung's four functions – sensation (earth), feeling (water), thinking (air) and intuitive (fire).

Empedocles (born c. 490 BCE) was the first to establish the four elements, although almost all ancient cosmologies have a similar fourfold arrangement, sometimes even a fifth – ether. The four elements were considered to make all the structures of the world and to flow through all of life. To Empedocles, elements in the things outside ourselves resonate with corresponding elements within us. Not quite 'As above, so below,' nor the ancient belief that all things in the universe are connected, but similar.

Some of today's astrologers maintain that the elements are not merely concepts but vital forces that make up creation. In this way, the elements are not only the primary building blocks of astrology but forces of energy which we respond to. Which is one explanation for how astrology works.

Another mechanism, which again has its roots in ancient philosophy (Pythagoras's Harmony of the Spheres), was put forward by Dr Percy Seymour in the mid-1980s. Seymour argues that Earth's magnetic field is affected by the sun and moon and the planets: it is as if 'the whole solar system is playing a symphony on Earth's magnetic field. We are all genetically tuned to receive a different set of melodies from this symphony.' Accordingly, as a baby develops in the womb its nervous system responds to these magnetic melodies which in turn synchronize with the internal biological clock, ultimately triggering the birth process.

This theory chimes with my belief – and it is just a belief – that we are born at a time when the sun, the moon and the planets reflect who we are. Being born at a particular time in a particular place is not a random event – we don't arrive in this world quite by chance and become stuck for life with a horoscope of that moment in

	ELEMENT	MODALITY
ARIES 20 MAR–19 APR	Fire	Cardinal
LEO 22 JUL–22 AUG	Fire	Fixed
SAGITTARIUS 22 NOV–21 DEC	Fire	Mutable
TAURUS 20 APR–20 MAY	Earth	Fixed
VIRGO 23 AUG–21 SEPT	Earth	Mutable
CAPRICORN 21 DEC–19 JAN	Earth	Cardinal
GEMINI 21 MAY–21 JUNE	Air	Mutable
LIBRA 22 SEP–22 OCT	Air	Cardinal
AQUARIUS 19 JAN–18 FEB	Air	Fixed
CANCER 22 JUN–20 JUL	Water	Cardinal
SCORPIO 23 OCT–21 NOV	Water	Fixed
PISCES 19 FEB–20 MAR	Water	Mutable

time: 'Ah, if only I'd been born a day later, my life would be totally different.'

The sun, the moon and the planets do not make us who we are. Neither do the sun and moon and the planets cause events. They mirror them.

My belief is not a million miles away from Jung's concept of synchronicity. 'Whatever is born or done at this moment of time, has the quality of this moment of time.' Accordingly, the positions of the sun, moon and planets do not directly influence the individual – they do not cause certain traits and drive events on Earth – but they coincide with them.

With or without a scientific framework to support it, astrology works. Millions upon millions of people across the world look to astrology for answers, and, clearly, they find them. Otherwise, astrology would have died out in the 17th century. Although I have offered my ideas about the 'stars' mirroring events in our lives and reflecting who we are, I am not entirely convinced that some kind of energetic principle is not at work. I say this because I have noticed that on days when a strong Saturn aspect is present I wake up uncharacteristically grumpy, feeling the weight of my worries and viewing pretty well everything through a negative lens. It passes within a day or two. This phenomenon, by the way, does not occur because I am already aware of the Saturn aspect, but when I feel the world is against me I turn to my ephemerides and sure enough there it is: Saturn.

I have developed a way of handling a Saturn transit, by the way, of actively embracing it rather than grumping away all day: I ask myself what it is that I am trying to avoid; what is playing a funeral march in the back of my mind, and once I have found it I deal with it.

Astrology is a living thing, whether you take this to mean it is an 'energetic force' or as relevant today as it was thousands upon thousands of years ago. What I have endeavoured to bring you here is an authentic but light-hearted view of the 12 signs of the zodiac in the workplace. I'm not the kind of astrologer who focuses only on the 'nicer' aspects of a sign but on the less agreeable qualities too. No one is perfect, and to a large extent it is our imperfectness that makes us human and certainly individuals.

I also hope I have inspired you to see astrology as a marvellous tool for understanding who we are and why we do what we do – both inside and outside the workplace – and to suspend disbelief even though we do not have a scientific explanation for how it works. Take it on trust from your QBE astrologer: it does work.

Enjoy!

THE
FIRE SIGNS
ARIES, LEO AND
SAGITTARIUS

THE ELEMENT FIRE

Before we get down to the nitty-gritty of the fire signs in the workplace, we need to understand the concept of the element: fire.

There are four elements in astrology – fire, earth, air and water[2] – and each element incorporates three signs. All element groups have a multitude of features in common, although there will be differences from sign to sign.

Think of fire. What comes to mind? Flickering flames in a log basket or a forest fire, out of control and destroying vast tracts of land? Fire can warm or it can burn you to a crisp. And so it is with the fire signs: they can bring warmth, humour and sheer brilliance to their endeavours, yet their incendiary natures can destroy their efforts and their relationships.

The discovery of fire, or more precisely the ability to make fire, was one of the most seminal achievements of early man. With the power to create fire came heat and light independent of nature and the time of year. Fire was also used to cook food, to clear the land for planting, to keep predators at bay and to forge tools and ceramic objects and ornaments. Fire also had a social function, being a focus for gatherings and beacon for travellers.

We can learn a lot about fire signs from this little foray into the Stone Age, not least that fiery Aries in particular has something of the cave-dweller about him or her! Fiery people are creative, resourceful, sociable and generous. Their warmth draws people toward them; they are beacons of information, ideas and activities

The elements and modalities are discussed in the section on *How Astrology Works.*

and the starting point for almost anything.

The psychologist, Carl Jung (a Leo) made several studies of astrology and likened his 'intuitive' function to the element, fire. The 'intuitive' type converts facts, details and concepts into larger pictures. 'Intuitives' define where something began and where it is going. They thrive on possibilities, atmosphere and opportunities. They look to the future, act on hunches and enjoy speculation.

Fire signs exude confidence and enthusiasm; they are dynamic, spontaneous and original.

Your typical fire sign approaches the world with a refreshing naivety. Aries, Leo and Sagittarius find adventure and drama around every corner. They can blag their way into and out of jobs, relationships and difficulties – most of the latter of their own making. They are energetic, strong, carefree, assertive, vital, frank and

loyal. They propel themselves through life with an enviable lack of concern for their safety, their old age and sometimes other people.

Fire signs are not reflective. Nor do they make good strategists. They prefer to intuit their way forward, relying on instinct to get the desired result. They're doers, not thinkers.

Now, this does not mean fiery people lack intelligence. What they tend to fall short on is foresight. They simply do not have time to put together a list of pros and cons and to perform the required research. (They would prefer to rely on others for that, although their secondary problem – a resistance to advice – means guidance is almost always ignored anyway.) They rush into situations without due thought, only to discover problems and drawbacks halfway through, resulting in many bruises, largely to their egos. Nonetheless, it is surprising how often this gung-ho attitude breeds success. Ah, well, fortune favours the fearless.

When we think of fire, we see flames. Flames rise and fall, change colour and intensity; they crackle and spit. Fire signs do not like standing still. They enjoy being on the move and require the stimulation of new places and new faces. They rise to a challenge and relish competition. When blocked or criticized they crackle and spit!

Patience is not a virtue in the fire camp; ambition drives Aries and Leo in particular, and even the more easy-going Sagittarian usually finds a place at the top table. But with impatience comes intolerance and fire signs can be very dismissive of those who are slower, less able and more reticent. They learn the hard way about the power of 'the quiet ones'.

Subtlety and innuendo are invariably lost on fiery folk. They themselves are incapable of artifice so they cannot detect it in others. This is both a plus and a minus: a plus because the carefully disguised insult rarely penetrates the veneer of their super self-confidence, yet on the minus side it makes them extremely easy to manipulate.

Aries, Leo and Sagittarius believe life should be simple. They expect to get from A to B in a direct line, and they become irritated by complications, detours and red tape. To their credit, you know where you stand with a fire sign and they endeavour to make life simple for others.

There are degrees of fieriness, however, and whether you are rocket fuel in a three-piece suit or sunset in a little black dress depends upon how many planets and points you have in fire besides the Sun in your birth chart.

FIRE ON A SCALE OF 1–10

If you are curious to know just how fiery you or your boss, colleague or employee are, you'll need a birth date and, ideally, also a time and place of birth. Whether you use an online service to tabulate the chart for you or you yourself have the knowledge, establishing the degree of heat is easy: add up all the planets and points in fire signs, according to the list below. It's simply a numbers game.

Ascendant = 3	Venus = 3	Saturn = 2
Sun = 3	Mars = 3	Uranus = 1
Moon = 3	Mid-heaven = 1	Neptune = 1
Mercury = 3	Jupiter = 2	Pluto = 1

Russell Brand: 9 points in fire.

If you score 9 points or more in fire signs, you are a true firebrand; between 5 and 8 you are hot, but not too hot to handle; between 1 and 4 and you're nice and toasty.

Even without the benefit of a chart to inform you just how fiery an individual is, you'll know by the behaviour. A surfeit of fire breeds over-aggressiveness, recklessness, impatience and intolerance; a manageable amount inspires confidence, leadership, courage and ingenuity. Even one planetary body in fire, as long as it rates 3, will provide drive, assurance, warmth and sociability.

Think of the actor-comedian Russell Brand and President Donald Trump: these two men epitomize the drama, supreme self-confidence and aggressiveness of fire. Both these men score 9 on the fire scale: Russell with the Moon, Mars and Jupiter in Aries and Neptune in Sagittarius; and Trump with Mars, Ascendant and Pluto in Leo and Moon in Sagittarius.

Helen Mirren and Angela Merkel both score 7 on the fire scale – Mirren with Mercury, the Sun and Pluto in Leo and Merkel with Mars and the Ascendant in Sagittarius and Pluto in Leo. Neither of these women has the brashness and ballsiness of a surfeit of fire, just enough to take them where they wanted to go – the top – and to keep them there.

Even having only the Sun in a fire sign can get you places. Author and philanthropist, J. K. Rowling, has nothing else in fire in her chart except the Sun in Leo. And look where that took her.

J. K. Rowling: 3 points in fire.

I should just mention that Joseph Stalin was born with the Sun and Venus in Sagittarius (6 on the fire scale) and Guy Fawkes, who tried to blow up the Houses of Parliament in 1605, had the Sun, Moon, Mercury and Venus in Aries (12 on the fire scale). Combustible indeed.

ARIES
IN THE WORKPLACE

20 MARCH–19 APRIL

Element: Fire
Modality: Cardinal
Ruling planet: Mars

CURRICULUM VITAE

At the vernal equinox on 21 March, the Sun enters Aries, and during the following 12 months works its way through the remaining 11 signs. Aries is thus the first sign of the zodiac, and in keeping with its pole position breeds a bunch of people who like to be first in the queue, individuals who like to win and believe they are the leaders of the pack.

All fire signs are spontaneous, creative and sociable, but Aries is a Cardinal[3] sign and the Cardinals are self-motivated and fiercely ambitious. It is this combination of fire and Cardinality that makes members of team Aries high-flyers and certainly contenders.

All well and good so far.

The downside to this sign is a serious shortfall in patience and persistence and a degree of

STRENGTHS
Courageous
Passionate
Confident
Enthusiastic
WEAKNESSES
Vengeful
Argumentative
Irascible
Bloody-minded

3   Cardinal is one of three modalities: see the section on *How Astrology Works.*

pig-headedness and wilfulness that often results in a failure to reach the heights of their expectations.

Arians are the sprinters of the zodiac, not the marathon runners.

Aries is ruled by Mars, the Greek god of war, which explains its assertive and fearless nature – the Martians can be a tad scary at times, and they're always ready for a fight. This is a physically strong sign – often athletically built and blessed with good muscle tone – and all Arians require an outlet for

their energy. An Aries who has gone to seed and become a couch potato is one who is dealing with a catalogue of failure.

Aries rules the head, which means this part of the body is both the weak spot and

its strong point: a weakness because Arians are prone to headaches and migraine (usually a response to stress), dental issues and facial damage and a strength because they can have great hair, a strong jawline, firm chin and an innate ability to put mind over matter.

THE ARIES BOSS

 As we can see from the Aries CV, this individual aspires to positions of power and authority, and, one way or another, he or she usually gets to the top. This does not necessarily make Arians good bosses, but they can make decisions – they're not ditherers. And given time and enough humbling experiences they can fulfil their leadership promise quite spectacularly.

Think for a moment of make-up mogul, Bobbie Brown, and the multi-millionaire host of *The Apprentice*, Alan Sugar, and publisher Hugh Hefner, he of the Playboy empire, Arians one and all.

Arians make excellent entrepreneurs. Indeed, they are far better managing their own businesses than trying to fit into a corporate straitjacket. Your Aries CEO

does not appreciate towing the party line or listening to advice. These bosses do not go in for endless boardroom discussions: meetings will be short and sweet and don't give them any details. They're big-picture people; that the devil is in the detail is for you (the underling) to worry about and for them to find out only if you haven't done your job.

This sign makes and breaks the rules.

The Aries boss is a force of nature. They appear to have an endless supply of energy. The truth is, Martians run out of gas fast and require frequent pit stops to operate at their best. Without short breaks, the Aries boss will become short-tempered and prone to making mistakes. They need protecting from themselves, which means you, as a colleague or employee, ensuring they are left alone in the sanctuary of their own space from time to time during a working day.

Arians are naturals when it comes to multi-tasking. They can channel their energies in ten directions at once, often leaving a trail of loose ends for others to snip. Until their mid-40s – the time of the Saturn and Uranus oppositions[4] – Arian bosses will tend to overcommit themselves, first because they cannot resist a challenge and second because they're often short of money. This is one of the most generous signs of the zodiac – there'll be impressive bonuses and rewards for employees –

but it's a sure sign of financial trouble when your Aries boss starts nit-picking about waste and turning down the heat/air-conditioning.

Sadly, bankruptcy is not uncommon in an Aries business.

Arguments are many in the Aries hot seat. Not only does this sign have a fragile

---

4   Between the ages of 42 and 46, Saturn opposes its natal position as does Uranus. This is invariably a time of crisis: roads run out and past mistakes come back to haunt us.

ego, but it treats every difference of opinion as a reason to go to war. Fortunately, nothing lasts long in Aries country, and one of the most endearing features of this sign is that it will admit its mistakes – and be the first to apologize.

Arian supreme self-confidence and enthusiasm inspire others to believe in them too. If you want to rescue an ailing company, call in an Aries and challenge him or her

to get it back on its feet. Aries loves the thrill of the mission, but once the company is up and running again, it's probably time to move on to fresh fields.

Aries is marvellous in short bursts, but runs out of steam in the long haul.

Another of Aries' problems when it comes to management is that he or she wants to be popular. To this end Mr or Ms Aries will be easy-going and amiable, even tolerant, at first. However, once members of staff begin to treat the Aries boss like an 'old mate' things begin to go downhill. The once affable boss becomes more demanding and instead of using the encouraging carrot to get the best out of employees, the stick comes out and orders and threats are issued instead. In this way the workplace becomes something of a battleground.

Fortunately, Aries learns by experience and learns quickly. As we know, fire signs don't listen to advice, but Aries is prepared to try new tactics. After a short war of attrition, your Martian boss is likely to gather together all members of the company and outline a new way forward. This may well be done at a team-building course, preferably with outdoorsy challenges – archery, quad bikes and adrenaline-boosting activities are Arian favourites.

The balance of power restored, the Aries boss can get on with the job of making the company a growing concern... that is, before he or she moves on to pastures new.

THE ARIES EMPLOYEE

Arians are not good in subsidiary roles. This you must understand if you plan to take on an Arian employee.

Of course, everyone has to start somewhere, even Mr and Ms Aries, but unless they are quickly promoted, they will not deliver of their best. A way around this as an employer is to give your Aries worker a degree of independence: a 'special' task that is only for him or her. When they feel highly regarded Arians up their game, but if they're criticized or down graded, they'll sulk, and most probably hand in their notice.

A nine-till-five routine will not suit Mr or Ms Aries. Nor do they appreciate being desk-bound. They cannot be placed in straitjackets of any kind. Please put them on flexitime. However, they are incredibly hard workers and given a deadline, they'll meet it, even if they've had to put in a couple of all-nighters.

You'll soon know when the rot has set in, so to speak, and your Aries employee is looking at the door marked 'Exit'. Your former eager beaver will start arriving a little later for work, and taking a little longer for lunch. And instead of leaping into the breach or volunteering for overtime, he or she will often be missing from view – in the cloakroom, the staff room, picking up a prescription – anywhere, in fact, other than the workbench.

Aries loves speed and performs most functions at a rate of knots. This is both a plus and a minus. If you ask for a task to be done by a specific time, it will be done. However, speed does not always guarantee perfection, and Aries is prone to the occasional slip-up. Fortunately, because the mission was accomplished way ahead of the deadline, there will be time to mop up spilled milk.

And then there's the famous Aries frankness. This sign really doesn't get subtlety.

They are honest to the point of rudeness. To many bosses and co-workers this is a virtue – you know exactly where you are with them and where they're coming from – but to more sensitive souls such candour is unacceptable. Your Aries employee is probably not the one you'll want to head a campaign that requires ample supplies of charm and flattery. Take it or leave it is the Aries way. Remember the caveman...

Aries responds to challenges and rewards. If a prize of some description is offered for the best piece of work or there is a competition between fellow workers, your Arian will pull out all the stops to win. And, yes, there'll be a bit of a sulk should they be pipped to the post. It won't last long, though. Aries quickly forgives and forgets, and is often left wondering why other people seem to be proffering a cold shoulder.

This is indeed one of the most competitive signs of the zodiac, which has its pluses in that you'll have a winning employee, but the downside is that a degree of friction will pervade the workplace.

Conflict and Aries are never far apart.

Somewhat paradoxically, Arians want to be popular and they love company. However, they are not truly team players. They can work in a team, but since they like their own way and believe in themselves so completely, some of the less outgoing and self-effacing members of the group can become resentful. If enough of the

group feel disenfranchised they'll band together and mount a mutiny.

One Aries client of mine – a TV presenter, talented and vivacious (9 on the fire scale) – was utterly bewildered when a colleague far less able, attractive and charismatic took her job. What my client had underestimated was the level of antagonism she had generated in the workplace by being inconsiderate and resistant to any kind of advice. And, of course, she was too consumed with her own agenda to appreciate the subtle hints being given by superiors and colleagues.

Aries never sees the writing on the wall.

Nonetheless, if you're looking to hire someone who can bring energy and innovation into your company, someone who will act with courage and candour, pick an Aries. Your workspace will be full of life and, given independence, praise and a mission, you'll be oh so glad you did.

ATHLETE

TEST/FIGHTER
PILOT

FORMULA ONE
DRIVER

FLIGHT
ATTENDANT

CAREERS FOR
MR OR MS
ARIES

SURGEON

DANGEROUS
SPORTS
ORGANIZER

MOUNTAIN
GUIDE/RESCUER

GYM
INSTRUCTOR

SPORTS
PRESENTER/
JOURNALIST/
PHYSIO

FIREMAN

LEO IN THE WORKPLACE

22 JULY–22 AUGUST

Element: Fire
Modality: Fixed
Ruling planet: the Sun

CURRICULUM VITAE

In Aries we found the raw energy and intense pace of fire; in Leo we meet the still centre of the flame. Due to its Fixed[5] modality, fiery Leo is constant, strong and true. Yet these self-same virtues sometimes turn into vices, and this sign can also be stubborn, resistant to change and domineering.

Ruled by the Sun, the star around which all the planets in the solar system revolve, Leos like to be centre stage, the pivot about which others rotate. They gravitate to the spotlight and expect to be worshipped and adored, and certainly never disrespected.

The brightest star in the constellation Leo is Regulus, the royal star, which goes a long way toward explaining why members of this sign have a regal bearing and quite naturally expect to be treated like monarchs. (Please do

STRENGTHS
Strong
Loyal
Firm
Determined

WEAKNESSES
High-handed
Bossy
Tunnel-visioned
Immovable

5   Cardinal, Fixed and Mutable make up the astrological modalities. Aries is Cardinal, Sagittarius Mutable and Leo is Fixed.

not forget this because even the most accommodating, self-effacing Leo is a star in his or her private universe.)

Think of high summer – the earth has grown warmer through the preceding three months and sustains its heat even when the weather is inclement. The corn stands tall, the grapes on the vine are plump and nature celebrates its richness and abundance.

Leo is a highly creative sign, warm, giving and opulent.

Leos bring colour and drama into every aspect of life, including the workspace.

They are performers and motivators, the beating heart of endeavours and the hub to which other people are irresistibly drawn.

The Sun, of course, is not only our source of heat, energy and light, but it also has the capacity to destroy us. Our star is a perpetual series of thermo-nuclear explosions; the parallel being that Leos have their dark side. Given enough provocation, they can eviscerate you!

Pride is their biggest downfall. Members of this sign aim to impress and, to their credit, they work incredibly hard to achieve their ends. They care about their image; they want always to be seen at their best and they will do everything in their power to be loved and treated as a superior being. Wound them, ignore them, fail to appreciate their offerings and, worse, humiliate them and they'll not only turn on you but themselves. (Scorpios are not the only members of the zodiac to self-destruct, the difference being that Leos do so in a blaze of glory.)

Oh, and while we're on the subject of the dark side, Leos have huge confidence in their own power. They radiate power. But you know what they say: 'power tends to corrupt and absolute power corrupts absolutely'.

Leo rules the heart and the circulatory system, which on the one hand, inspires them to do everything with heart, but when faced with failure or rejection they can feel a physical pain in their heart. They are truly all heart.

THE LEO BOSS

See that woman over there? The one with the billowing mane of hair; the one in the Victoria Beckham trouser suit and the Manolo Blahnik stilettoes. And who is that distinguished man being fast-tracked through airport security by a uniformed employee? You may not know their names or why exactly they turn heads, but you can be sure they belong to the Leo club.

This is a club to which only the elite gain entry.

And while we're on the subject of clubs and airports, Leo bosses really don't do economy: it's club class all the way; better still, first class. Extravagance comes naturally to Leo.

Leos run a company like a sovereign state. They believe in pecking orders and formalities; rules, regulations and tradition. There will be rituals, whether these are procedures that must be followed (or else) or annual get-togethers that everyone is expected to attend. And most Leo bosses like to dress up for the occasion. And while not every Leo CEO is a fashion plate, almost all of them have a sense of style.

Think for a moment of the lion, the king of the jungle. Lions lie around a lot, basking in the sun, but they are not idle: they are watching and waiting, and when they see something they want, they'll pounce. There's a lot you can learn about the Leo boss from his animal counterpart. He or she may do a lot of lounging around and may appear indifferent to the goings-on of the workplace; there may be long lunches and frequent absences. But Leo CEOs know exactly what's going on; if they like what they see there will be big rewards, and if they don't, you're fired!

Leos like to be surrounded by positive people; staff who are smiley and energetic;

people who reflect Leo's glory. This sign has a complete disregard for weakness or misery, which is why it is never a good idea to fall on your boss's mercy. He or she respects strength and commitment in others. If you're whinging and whining, you have to leave.

Leos are born to rule; they like to be in charge, to order people around. When they're feeling successful and appreciated they are the most generous and benign of commanders-in-chief, but when things go wrong, the dark side of the sign emerges. Leos may be slow to anger but once they blow, they blow. And heads will roll. If you make a cardinal error, you can expect to be punished, and the more fear you show the worse the punishment will be. This is a characteristic that must be understood if you are to thrive in a Leo-ruled company.

While a Leo boss expects to be venerated, there is a fine line between respect and obsequiousness. If you overdo the toadying, you'll be held in contempt and if you treat your boss as an equal you'll be sent to the colonies. There's only room for one boss.

Never question your Leo CEO; you are there to follow orders. Of course, if those orders turn out to be wrong, you'll get the blame. Likewise, the Leo boss will claim the credit for a job well done by you.

Getting your way with Mr or Ms Leo requires shrewdness. (Never allow them to spot an artful device, though.) Agree with everything your Leo boss says,

follow every directive, but quietly drop in a suggestion disguised as a mere splash in a stream of consciousness; later congratulate him or her on coming up with such a brilliant idea. Flattery is your ace. Once you have proved your loyalty, your Leo boss will allow you a little more autonomy, but you must never forget your place in the pecking order.

Now, before you run away with the notion that Leo bosses are to be avoided at all costs, you are, by and large, in a safe pair of hands. This sign has courage and strength; when the chips are down Leos will mount a plan and carry it out successfully. They will not be intimidated; they will never give up or give in. And it is the combination of toughness and persistence that wins the day, a combination which breeds respect.

And, you know, there's something innately reassuring about being in the company of a boss who has unquestioning faith in his own omnipotence.

THE LEO EMPLOYEE

 Let's be clear, Leos are not subservient to anyone. So, if you're planning to hire a member of this royal sign, remind yourself that no matter how meek and obliging the interviewee may appear, secretly he or she wants to run the company, or at least part of it. However, you should also bear in mind that your prospective Leo employee will be worth every penny of his or her salary – you're hiring a star performer.

Leos carry out any task with heart and skill and, most importantly, in style.

Another great plus with this sign is its members have a strong sense of responsibility. They get the job done. They might not be the first people to volunteer for a risky enterprise, particularly one that could jeopardize their image, but they will put themselves forward if they can see the task could lead to promotion, and they rarely miss a chance to show their leadership potential.

Leos are great team players as long as they can be leader. They can become very snarky if forced to take orders from those they believe they are superior to. But since not everyone in an organization wants to take on the burden of leadership, why not give your Leo the opportunity to prove his or her worth? This sign is brilliant at telling other people what to do and organizing anything from an office outing to a political campaign.

Always give your Leo employee credit where credit is due and pile on the praise and approbation, especially in front of other staff members. (Leos thrive in front of an audience.) While a bonus or salary increase is always welcome – this sign has a taste for the expensive and often runs into cash-flow crises – what is even more appreciated is a raise in status: a title of some description, a plaque on the wall, a special task that sets him or her apart from colleagues.

Leos have more patience than their fellow fire signs: their Fixed natures allow them to persist until the job is done and they can withstand all manner of setbacks. Faced with a problem, Leos will carefully look for a loophole, then marshal their resources, which can include calling in

favours from past connections and a serious charm offensive, and fight back. They are not opposed to the use of barter and emotional blackmail to achieve their ends.

A lot of pouting and mane-tossing goes on when Leos are denied.

At the very core of your Leo employee is a rock-solid conviction of his or her own self-worth. Indeed, Leos' faith in themselves is far stronger than their belief in others. They are a naturally sceptical bunch of people. They may be friendly

and warm, but they don't give their trust easily. Indeed, the aloofness that so many Leos exude has far more to do with a lack of trust than any innate snobbishness.

The Leo employee almost always has a grand plan for his or her future broken down in one-, five- and ten-year stages, and they stick to the plan, regardless. They find it difficult to admit defeat, which can mean they hang on to hope and

ambition even when they would be far better diversifying.

Digging their toes in is an occupational hazard for Leos.

Leos do not like owning up to their mistakes. They will go to uncommon lengths to avoid acknowledging any guilt. If you are seeking an apology, you'll wait a long time, and the war of attrition will wear everyone down, except Mr or Ms Leo.

Members of this sign do not appreciate change, especially change which is thrust upon them. They would rather beat their heads against a proverbial brick wall than give in to an unbidden change. Of course, even they know the old chestnut – there can be no growth without change – so they can and will alter their course, but only in the wake of a fair warning and a long period of adjustment.

On balance Leos' virtues outweigh their vices. They are a force to be reckoned with in a company, and unless they are treated very, very badly, they will reward you with long and loyal service – and along the way you'll have plenty of fun.

They are worth their weight in gold.

MOTIVATIONAL SPEAKER

STYLIST

HEAD-HUNTER

FASHION EDITOR/DESIGNER

PRODUCER/ DIRECTOR

CAREERS FOR MR OR MS LEO

HAIRDRESSER

THEATRICAL AGENT

HEART SPECIALIST

TV PRESENTER

ACTOR

SAGITTARIUS IN THE WORKPLACE

22 NOVEMBER–21 DECEMBER

Element: Fire
Modality: Mutable
Ruling planet: Jupiter

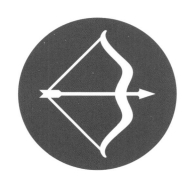

CURRICULUM VITAE

With Aries we had ignition, with Leo radiation and in Sagittarius we find convection – the spread of fire, the reach of fire. In keeping with its Mutable[6] modality, Sagittarius is associated with travel, and the dissemination of knowledge and information.

This is a sign that is difficult to contain; it requires freedom, independence and limitless possibilities.

Ruled by Jupiter, the largest planet in the solar system, and in myth the king of the gods, Sagittarians kowtow to no one; they are above the law, they follow their own star. Unlike Leo who is a natural ruler, Sagittarius has no time for pomp and circumstance, rules and red tape; it is a sign that needs to be unfettered by responsibilities and commitments. That doesn't mean, of course, that Jupiter people don't enjoy being seen and admired. No indeed.

STRENGTHS
Optimistic
Impartial
Magnanimous
Adaptable

WEAKNESSES
Unable to commit
Careless
Tactless
Unfocused

6   Mutable signs – Virgo, Pisces, Gemini and Sagittarius – are ambiguous and diffusive.

The Sun enters Sagittarius just before Thanksgiving and leaves a few days before Christmas, thereby covering an entire season of celebration. The 'holidays' are a consumer-fest, an extravagance of riches, a feast in every sense of the word. This period of the year also has religious significance for a large swathe of the world's population.

All the above is quintessentially Sagittarian. Members of this sign live life to the full and rarely think of the cost of their extravagances, whether in terms of money or health and well-being; they may not belong to an orthodox religion, but they are innately spiritual. They turn to a higher power for guidance and salvation, and put a philosophical twist on every setback. And, perhaps because of their optimism and belief that 'it's all good', Sagittarians are some of the most popular and successful people on the planet.

Think for a moment, though, of the symbol for Sagittarius – the Centaur, half man, half horse. In myth, centaurs were a wild bunch of individuals, prone to drunken brawls and indulging in the pleasures of the senses. Yet one of their number, Chiron,

was a revered teacher and healer. Here we see the two sides of Sagittarius: the lover of excess and the purveyor of wisdom and knowledge.

Can we talk thunder and lightning? Jupiter, king of the gods, was largely a benign fellow, but when things went pear-shaped and mere mortals got out of line, he hurled thunderbolts at the offenders. His anger was short-lived, however. And so it is with Sagittarius. For nine-tenths of the time they are the greatest people to have around, but provoke them, especially if they're hungover or exhausted, and you'll need to run for cover. Fortunately, by the time you surface Mr or Ms Sagittarius will be over it.

Sagittarians forgive and forget.

THE SAGITTARIAN BOSS

Welcome to the rodeo! The Sagittarian boss tends to run his company like a circus: his staff a cast of diverse characters and he the ringmaster. There'll be days when there's a lot of clowning around; days when scary events occur; and days when the circus grinds to a halt due to unforeseen circumstances. (Sagittarians can forget the little things in life like paying company tax on time, renewing licences, or even locking the door upon leaving. They find red tape irritating in the extreme.)

The above may be a tad tongue-in-cheek, but Sagittarius dances to its own drum.

The Sagittarian boss does not place himself at a distance from his or her staff. Celestial Centaurs are accessible and friendly. They like to have a finger in every pie and they make themselves as available to employees on the lowest rung of the corporate ladder as those at the very top. They leave a warm breeze in their wake as they canter through the corridors, waving and nodding at the worker bees.

Sagittarians do indeed prefer to move fast; not only because they enjoy speed, but because they over-pile their plates; they have far too many people to see and places to go. They take multi-tasking to a whole new level, and in the process forget essential details and make unnecessary errors. Fortunately, because they inspire such love and loyalty, their staff dig them out of holes, often before anyone outside the business discovers the mistake.

The great strength of the Sagittarian boss lies in his or her vision. These are broad-brushstroke people. They see the potential in an idea and can inspire others to believe in it too. They themselves may not oversee the project step by step – that's what the worker bees are for – but their faith, enthusiasm and vision will carry it through. Sagittarians can grasp complicated issues with ease, breaking them down to the simplest principles.

The Jupiterian boss invariably has intellectual aspirations. He or she will be well-informed and up-to-date on everything from the latest technology to the current best-seller. Indeed, if you are being interviewed by a Sagittarian employer, the way to his or her heart and a job is to steer the discussion toward what rock bands you're into/films you've just seen/political controversy that's just been unearthed.

By the way, if you have thin skin, the Sagittarian boss is not a good fit for you. This sign is very outspoken. You'll be in no doubt as to what is on his or her mind and how much you are appreciated, or not, as the case may be.

The celestial Centaur sees his company as a team. He or she may be the ringmaster, but Sagittarians do not put themselves above others: they pool ideas, encourage innovation and even enjoy an argument. They are generous with praise, generous with financial rewards and prepared to give people a second chance.

Ninety per cent of the time your Sagittarian boss is a sunny, warm-hearted, amusing person, but that remaining ten per cent requires you to come to work with an asbestos suit in your backpack. Just in case. What will evoke a Jupiterian's wrath are lies, cheating and unfair play. And when Mr or Ms Sagittarius gets mad, those mythical thunderbolts are released. Your only hope if you're in the line of fire is that your boss will soon be over it.

Sagittarians are quick to apologize and not averse to reinstating a fired employee.

While not every day in Sagittarius land will be fun on sticks, there will be plenty of good times. This sun sign loves to travel and finds as many excuses as possible to get away to distant locations. There should be company outings to far-off places – for team-building purposes, of course – and office meetings could be held in culturally diverse restaurants and bars. As for in-house cuisine, forget cheese and ham sandwiches: sushi, dim sum and pho are more likely to be on the menu.

You see, your Sagittarian boss is a citizen of the world, and he or she is only too happy for you to join in the adventure of it all.

THE SAGITTARIAN EMPLOYEE

If you are looking for an employee who will obey the rule book, someone who will be where you expect at any given moment and never volunteer an opinion if it differs from the company line, a follower, a pen-pusher, then please do not hire a Sagittarian. The only pen this employee will push is one that is fashioned into a missile and launched across the office and out of the window. On the other hand, if you are searching for someone to inspire the team – inspire you – and you like to see a bright and breezy staff member virtually every day of the working week, then employ Mr and Ms Sagittarius immediately, before some other organization pips you to the post.

Sagittarians have the most upbeat attitude in the zodiac. They will put a positive spin on almost any development, and it is extremely hard to crush their optimism and good nature. Only if they are burnt out and not at all well will you be confronted by a grumpy, uncooperative employee.

These individuals have boundless energy, and they can also drum up ideas and solutions to the most complex conundrums. In part, this is because they are natural problem-solvers but also because they spend a lot of time surfing/reading/watching documentaries and engaging in conversation with virtually anyone who

might cross their path. They may not all have the intellectual capacity of Einstein (who incidentally had the Moon in Sagittarius), but they will have deep pools of information from which they can draw when the occasion calls for it.

They work hard and play hard.

Your Sagittarian employee is not overtly ambitious; he or she won't be knocking at your door demanding promotion. However, this does not mean he or she does not have aspirations. These are the seekers of the zodiac, the people who enjoy the thrill of the quest and like nothing better than to be on a mission of some description. To get the best out of your Sagittarian employee, give him or her a  task that involves investigation and trips and meetings beyond the workplace. A desk-bound Sagittarian is not a happy camper.

These are not the diplomats of the zodiac, either: they call it as they see it, and they cannot disguise their feelings. They are also not the types to approve of sharp business practices; they will not abide deviousness and despise those who take advantage of others. Sagittarians will walk out of a well-paid job that they love should their integrity be compromised. Prepare to be put to shame by your Sagittarian employee, should you fall off the truth wagon.

One thing you need to know above all else about Sagittarians is that they have a deep-seated fear of commitment. Aside from this sign suffering from the 'runaway bride' syndrome, their CVs can turn into small novels. An innate restlessness is partly responsible for their impressive job turnover, but the main reason behind their reluctance to commit is a fear that they will be limiting their options, narrowing their horizons. Faced with a long-term obligation, their minds run through a series of 'inevitable' events leading to the demise of the relationship/job/purchase: a process which can prevent them from fulfilling their bright potential.

Sagittarians do better on short-term contracts and flexitime.

Needless to say, Jupiterians are repelled by boundaries of any description. They might be able to work to a deadline – in fact, they can produce their best when under the hammer of time – but they will not respond to rigid guidelines set by others. Like a racehorse, he or she needs a loose rein to function at their top level.

While there are drawbacks to every sign of the zodiac when it comes to working in a small or large group, Sagittarius is your guy. He (or she) will be popular with colleagues and superiors alike, and even if he puts his foot in it on occasion, his good humour and generous spirit more than makes up for any minor crimes and misdemeanours.

Sagittarians are jolly good fellows.

SPORTSMAN

SCHOLAR

AIRLINE PILOT/
CAPTAIN

GAMING
PROFESSIONAL

INTERPRETER

CAREERS FOR
MR OR MS
SAGITTARIUS

COMEDY ACTOR/
WRITER

IMPORT/
EXPORT EXECUTIVE

TRAVEL AGENT

YOGA TEACHER/
REIKI MASTER

MENTOR

INTER-RELATIONSHIPS
Who gets on with whom in the workplace

FIRE-FIRE

As a general rule of thumb, fire signs get on pretty well with each other. Aries, Leo and Sagittarius are all fiercely individual, but they have respect for their element fellows who display the same courage, feistiness and ingenuity as themselves.

All fire signs need to follow their passion and to have fun while doing the job. And a

fire workplace will be thrumming with activity and high spirits.

You get serious productivity with a fire crew. They're all energetic and motivated, although Aries and Sagittarius can become bored easily, and when a project begins to stumble they tend to move on to more rewarding challenges. Leo is the sign with the tenacity and commitment.

An ideal combination, therefore, an ideal balance, is Aries with Leo, and Sagittarius with Leo: that way you acquire all the fire power necessary to get an endeavour off the ground, plus the staying power to see it through to the end.

Fire/fire combinations hit it off brilliantly to begin with, but once the lustre has worn off, there can be arguments and hostilities. Fortunately, upsets do not last long, especially for Aries and Sagittarius, and even Leo can be brought round with liberal amounts of praise, flattery and nicely wrapped gifts.

Fighting for dominance can be a problem too, especially with Aries and Leo. These two are both signs of leadership and there will be considerable jockeying for position. Sagittarians, as we know, dance to their own tune and couldn't give a damn about being the boss. They do like the higher salary, though.

Extravagance and a loose grasp on economics could be the biggest problem posed by a predominantly fire team. Leo may try its hardest to bring the other two into line with spending, but Leo has its weak spot for luxury and really cannot exist in an environment where there is evidence of too much cost-cutting. So it's almost always a case of stones and glass houses.

Fire/fire combinations are best suited to businesses that demand showmanship, flair and creativity: sports, entertainment, advertising, travel, fashion, high-risk ventures and start-ups. You wouldn't want a bunch of fiery people working in an accounts office or a funeral parlour.

FIRE-EARTH

Fire and earth is not an easy mix. Fire scorches earth while earth puts out fire. These two groups have totally different agendas, totally different personalities. This does not mean, however, that they have nothing to offer one another in the workplace: it's just going to be a bumpy ride.

While Aries, Leo and Sagittarius like to get on with the job as soon as possible, flying by the seat of their pants, Taurus, Virgo and Capricorn require considerable time to think through a project and mount a strategy. Thus, fire gets enormously frustrated with earth and earth exasperated by fire.

The fire signs also tend to view the earth signs as

a rather dull crew while earthy Taurus, Virgo and Capricorn perceive their fiery colleagues and superiors as slightly superficial and childish.

However, there are advantages to earth/fire workplaces. Indeed, there is a name for this sun-sign combination – the steamroller. Fire's irresistible force and optimism

and earth's tenacity, strategy and realism make for an extremely powerful working relationship. They just won't want to go off to the same pub after work.

The dynamic between fire and earth is especially potent when they share a modality. A fire-earth relationship involving Aries and Capricorn, Leo and Taurus and Sagittarius and Virgo characterize the best and worst of the steamroller. The reason being that although they operate at different speeds and with contrasting mechanisms, they have a core connection. And that core connection is their shared modality. Sharing a modality is akin to belonging to the same family, but, like a family, they may not always function well as a unit. Sun signs that are 90 degrees away from each other have a dysfunctional relationship.

The secret to working well together whatever the fire/earth sign mix is that fiery people need to appreciate the value of caution and foresight and must cease to expect their earthy colleagues to deal with all the humdrum aspects of business. Earthy people, on the other hand, must acknowledge the importance of seizing the moment and recognize where they are unnecessarily using blocking and delaying tactics.

FIRE–AIR

Fire warms air while air fans the flames. A workplace with a good mix of fire signs and air signs is a company made in heaven. This is an ideal combination.

Fiery Aries, Leo and Sagittarius

and airy Gemini, Libra and Aquarius are positive and outgoing signs. They have little time for angst and cannot exist in an environment where there is back-biting and low ceilings – the latter literally and metaphorically. They rub along well together and bring out each other's best qualities.

Here you have the combined power of rational thought and intuitive action.

Air can analyse the probable outcomes of fire's ambitions without squashing its enthusiasm while fire can encourage airy people to get their ideas off the ground without giving them too much time to change their minds.

The benefit of a team nicely balanced between air and fire is that there is little conflict. Yes, there may be stimulating arguments and occasional rank disagreements but nothing to frighten the horses. They meet their problems with the intention of finding solutions, and find them they will.

If there is a downside to a fire/air group, it is that sometimes they get carried away with the glorious potential of a project and fail to dot the Is and cross the Ts. And, as we all know, the devil's in the detail.

Some fire and air combinations work better than others; the reason being one of the air signs will be a fire sign's opposite number. Put another way, an Aries-Libra combination, a Leo-Aquarius mix and a Sagittarius-Gemini team belong on opposite sides of the zodiac, and opposites both attract and repel. So, although you still have the winning combination of fire and air, there can be a little extra tension between opposite signs.

A workplace strong on air and fire is suited to businesses that involve ideas and action: news organizations, publishers, advertising companies, head-hunting establishments and companies concerned with travel and transportation.

FIRE-WATER

What happens when you pour water on fire? It goes out. And what happens when fire heats up water? It evaporates. Then again, steam heat is a force to be reckoned with. And where would we be without central heating? This is not an irredeemable combination but it takes a lot of work.

In the same way that fire and earth are elemental mismatches, so are fire and water. While both fire signs and water signs are driven by their emotions and instincts,

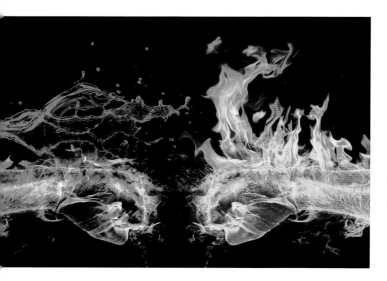

there is a tremendous difference in their basic temperaments. Fire signs are initiators; they don't need a lot of prodding and coaxing to bring their talents into the workplace. Water signs, on the other hand, require nurturing, encouragement and sensitive handling.

Aries, Leo and Sagittarius can be a tad too pushy and insensitive for Cancer, Scorpio and Pisces. When things go wrong, fire signs move onward and upward, working on the principle that eventually everyone will get over it and the next big thing will be the best big thing ever; water signs sulk and brood and silently plan payback. Thus, fiery folk are always shaken to the gills when the water sign they had considered no threat gets the promotion or rights a wrong for which the powers that be are forever in his or her debt.

Still waters run a little too deep for fire signs.

The way to get the best out of your water/fire team is to hold weekly in-house meetings to discuss issues and 'share'. (This might be irritating in the extreme for the fire signs, but it will work wonders for better office relations.) The sharing session should be held after an alcohol-free lunch. Fire gets animated on alcohol; water gets wistful.

Not all fire/water combinations are equal, however. Signs that are 90 degrees apart belong to the same modality, which tends to make for even more tension between them. Aries and Cancer, Leo and Scorpio and Sagittarius and Pisces have to work even harder on their relationship. Then again, the rewards are even greater.

STAR RATING BETWEEN ARIES, LEO AND SAGITTARIUS AND THE REST OF THE ZODIAC

	ARIES	LEO	SAGITTARIUS
ARIES	★ ★ ★ ★	★ ★ ★ ★	★ ★ ★ ★
TAURUS	★	★	★
GEMINI	★ ★ ★ ★ ★	★ ★ ★ ★ ★	★ ★ ★ ★
CANCER	★	★	★
LEO	★ ★ ★ ★	★ ★ ★ ★	★ ★ ★ ★
VIRGO	★	★	★
LIBRA	★ ★ ★ ★	★ ★ ★ ★ ★	★ ★ ★ ★ ★
SCORPIO	★ ★	★	★
SAGITTARIUS	★ ★ ★ ★	★ ★ ★ ★	★ ★ ★ ★
CAPRICORN	★	★	★
AQUARIUS	★ ★ ★ ★ ★	★ ★ ★ ★	★ ★ ★ ★ ★
PISCES	★	★	★ ★

THE
EARTH SIGNS
TAURUS, VIRGO
AND CAPRICORN

THE ELEMENT EARTH

Of all the building blocks in astrology, the elements take precedence. In the preceding section we explored fire – its nature, how fire types behave in the workplace, their potential as employees and employers and what careers suit them; now we come to earth – fire's polar opposite.

Earth is the most stable of the elements. In the same way that planet Earth revolves around the Sun in ellipses of approximately 365 days, yielding four seasons, 12 months and day and night, earth signs are predictable, reliable and consistent.

Earth signs are attuned to their physical senses; they want to be able to see something, touch it and know its component parts. They realize they live in a material world and instinctively understand how to manage it. Earth signs do not need to be told to earn a living and find a roof over their heads; it's second nature to them. They rely on reason; they are practically minded; they have patience, persistence and self-discipline.

You know where you are with the earth signs.

While fire corresponds to the Intuitive Function in Jungian psychology, earth relates to Sensation. Earth signs trust the concrete and the tangible: they mistrust spontaneity and rarely rush into anything. This element takes its time. Ideas and concepts have a place in earth world, but they're tucked away in the basement along with intuitions, dreams and the ephemeral things of life.

Such phrases as 'down to earth' and 'salt of the earth' are a good fit with Taurus, Virgo and Capricorn. These signs act responsibly; they follow the rules; they understand the importance of tradition and they prefer to remain in their comfort zone. To this end, they can strike some people as dull, unenterprising stick-in-the-muds.

Inasmuch as we rely on the Earth to nourish, sustain and support us, it cannot be taken for granted. When those tectonic plates clash, the resulting earthquake can be devastating; and when earth signs have been trampled on, dissed and generally abused, the payback can be very unpleasant indeed. Admittedly, it takes a long time before earth signs will run out of patience or give in to frustration, but when they're done, they're done.

Achievement and ambition are not the same: earth signs, with the exception of Capricorn, are rarely ruthlessly ambitious, but it is vitally important to them to achieve what they set out to do. And this can apply to anything from losing weight and acquiring a six-pack to taking on a personal or professional commitment and seeing it through to completion. Earth signs cannot accept failure in themselves, and they have very little tolerance for others who fail in their endeavours.

Earth signs are builders – sometimes quite literally since many of them work in the construction industry, become architects and engineers. However, the concept of building refers to the earth signs' ability to take something from its smallest beginnings and grow it into a solid and durable structure. If you want anything to last and withstand the ravages of time, get an earth sign on the job.

Earth signs tend to be the conformists and reactionaries of the zodiac, with the exception of Virgo, who is more adaptable and disinclined to nail his or her colours to any particular mast. For earthy people, history informs the future: knowing where you've come from is a reliable indicator of where you're going. This regard for the past, combined with a respect for law and order, makes them exemplary citizens: they pay their taxes and their bills, and honour their commitments and their elders. They believe in the institution of marriage and the need to father the next generation. Duty comes naturally to them.

If it weren't for the earth signs, chaos would rule.

Taurus, Virgo and Capricorn gravitate to roles which require that they organize, direct and advise. If you're in a group and someone has a clipboard and a stopwatch, it's sure to be an earth sign. These people get things done and they're not going to be deterred by opposition and emotional scenes.

The problem with the earth group is that its members can be impervious to other people's feelings, believing that what is right and proper, what has proved itself over time, should carry the day. They dig their toes in and get in the way of a whole lot of dreams and possibilities, even their own. Taurus, Capricorn and Virgo do not like to be argued with or undermined and they will do everything in their power to block and delay something that does not have their approval. They do not care how long it takes to prove a point.

To this end, earth signs can be extremely hard work whether you're working with them, living with them or sitting next to them on a transatlantic flight! Nonetheless, if something goes wrong, if something needs fixing, it's an earth sign who's going to put it right.

There are degrees of earthiness, however, and whether you are granite in a three-piece suit or titanium in a fluffy sweater depends upon how many planets and points you have in earth besides the Sun in your birth chart.

EARTH ON A SCALE OF 1-10

If you are curious to know just how earthy you or your boss, colleague or employee are, you'll need a birth date and, ideally, also a time and place of birth. Whether you use an online service to tabulate the chart for you or you yourself have the knowledge, establishing the degree of heat is easy: add up all the planets and points in earth signs, according to the list below. It's simply a numbers game.

Ascendant = 3   Venus = 3   Saturn = 2
Sun = 3   Mars = 3   Uranus = 1
Moon = 3   Mid-heaven = 1   Neptune = 1
Mercury = 3   Jupiter = 2   Pluto = 1

If you score 9 points or more in earth signs, you are a true rock of ages and nothing can budge you; between 5 and 8 you are solid, but semi-permeable; between 1 and 4 and your feet may be in a material world but your eyes are gazing at the stars.

Even without the benefit of a chart to inform you just how earthy an individual is, you'll know by the behaviour. A surfeit of earth breeds inflexibility, over-dominance, lack of compassion and self-righteousness; a manageable amount inspires self-reliance, pragmatism and forbearance. Even one planetary body in earth, if it rates a three, will provide patience, carefulness and reliability.

The earthy rock of ages is exemplified by many leaders and captains of industry: Martin Luther King – 'We are not makers of history. We are made by history' – was a Capricorn with a total of ten points in earth signs; footballer, entrepreneur and philanthropist David Beckham is a Sun Taurus with a total of 13 points

David Beckham: 13 points in earth.

Queen Elizabeth II: 6 points in earth.

in earth signs; and Warren Buffett, magnate, investor and philanthropist, is a Sun Virgo with six points in earth.

Earth signs predominate in both Queen Elizabeth I's and Queen Elizabeth II's charts – two of the greatest and longest-lived queens of England. Queen Elizabeth I was a Sun Virgo with a total of nine points in earth and Queen Elizabeth II is a Sun Taurus with six points in earth, although she acquires a further three for having Saturn conjunct her Mid-heaven. Cosmetic queens, Elizabeth Arden and Helena Rubenstein also rate high on the earth scale – nine points for Arden and 11 for Rubenstein.

But before you get carried away with the idea that a plethora of earth signs is God's gift to humanity, there are some other names in the hall of fame that resonate with the less glorious aspects of a surfeit of earth: Oliver Cromwell was a Sun Taurus with 12 points in earth, and Kim Jong-un is a Capricorn with six points in earth.

TAURUS IN THE WORKPLACE

20 APRIL–20 MAY

Element: Earth
Modality: Fixed
Ruling planet: Venus

CURRICULUM VITAE

Taurus, the first of the earth signs, comes in as spring reaches its zenith: the blossom hanging heavy on the trees bears the promise of fruit later in the year during the time of Virgo. Taurus therefore resonates with the riches of the earth; and, ruled by Venus, the planet of love, beauty and finance, this sign is also associated with sensuality, self-indulgence, abundance and acquisitiveness.

Taurus people enjoy the good things in life; they require security, stability and are highly resistant to change. They are also the most intractable of the earth signs. The reason for the celestial Bull's stubbornness and its dislike of change is its Fixed[7] modality. All the Fixed signs like to be in control but with Scorpio this tendency is moderated by its fluid watery nature, in Leo by its impatient fiery temperament and in Aquarius through the

STRENGTHS
Patient
Persistent
Loyal
Consistent

WEAKNESSES
Possessive
Pig-headed
Greedy
Obstructive

Fixed is one of the modalities: see the section on *How Astrology Works*.

Barbra Streisand: Sun in Taurus.

lightness of its airy being. Fixed and earth is about as immoveable as it gets.

When Taureans dig their toes in, you might as well give up and go home.

Taureans are interested in growth; they are not concerned with making it to the top of the tree, but when they do, which is surprisingly often, it will have been a by-product of consistent effort and sheer doggedness. Give this sign a job that provides a salary linked to the rate of inflation, a generous pension and three weeks' paid holiday a year, and you'll have a very contented member of staff.

The part of the body ruled by Taurus is the neck, which is why many Taureans have a strong neck and are prone to sore throats and tonsillitis. (Please keep the office space free from draughts.) They also often have beautiful voices and enjoy music – Dame Nellie Melba, Barbra Streisand, Adele, Sam Smith, Roy Orbison and Bing Crosby are Taureans all. And it is surprising how many dancers belong to team Taurus – Margot Fonteyn, Shirley MacLaine, Darcey Bussell and Natalia Osipova.

Never judge a Taurus by appearance: behind that placid, pleasant demeanour is someone who never gives up and never gives in.

THE TAURUS BOSS

Taurus loves comfort – comfort food, comfortable chairs, familiar faces, familiar places. He or she is in no rush; whether it's a business lunch or a boardroom discussion it's going to take time. Turn off your mobile phones and your iPads.

The Taurus boss is unlikely to come across as a high-flyer. He (or she) will appear unassuming and unthreatening; wealth will not be in evidence in his apparel or accoutrements, even if he's a billionaire. Think Taurean Mark Zuckerberg for a moment. Taureans are, however, rather conventional and believe in dressing correctly for the job – see-through tops and threadbare jeans won't go down at all well in an insurance office, no matter how brilliant you may be.

The workplace will be anything but ostentatious, although it will be pleasant. Ideally, there will be access to food and beverages, whether the premises are next to a great eatery or there are facilities for cooking and dining in-house. And there will be a store of favourite foods near at hand – in the desk drawer, the filing cabinet or a small fridge. And if you need to make a good impression, bring a sweet treat to the

meeting. Taureans are quite the foodies of the zodiac. They have an especially sweet tooth.

These earth-sign bosses will always get what they want. They'll listen patiently to your suggestions and demands, even appear to be in agreement, but unless they are 100 per cent behind a project or you, they won't yield an inch. They rely on past strategies which give guaranteed results, and only when one of those strategies fails to work will they consider a new one; even then, it's like pulling teeth.

Taureans can be impressed with a well-thought-out, well-researched idea, though, especially if they can see it will make money. Come prepared with all the facts and figures, and know the answer to every question before you make your pitch.

Whether your Taurus boss is a CEO of a corporation, the owner of a food truck or the director of an actors' studio there's a let's-roll-up-our-sleeves-and-get-on-with-it attitude to business. She (or he) will put in long hours to get a project off the ground and nurture it to completion, and she will expect the same commitment from you.

Quick fixes, get-rich-quick schemes and a fast track to the top are not the Taurus way. If you're ambitious and impatient for success, you're not a good fit for this

boss. It has taken years of effort and struggle for him or her to get there, and your Taurus boss expects you to do the same.

Since this earth sign is ruled by sweet Venus, it can sometimes be very difficult to establish that Mr or Ms Taurus is not only dissatisfied with you but ready to fire you. If at all possible the Taurus boss will have someone else do the dirty work, but once he or she has reached that decision, there'll be no point trying to alter it. You will, however, be given a fair settlement.

Which brings me on to the issue of unfair dismissal or unjust treatment. Taking your Taurus boss to an industrial tribunal will almost always end badly for you. Accept an offer the moment it is given. The only winner in a war of attrition will be Mr or Ms Taurus. And that goes for any difference of opinion.

The Taurus boss will expect and reward loyalty. This sign may watch every penny, but its members generously reward consistently good work and fidelity. And, rather like their opposite sign, the Scorpios, if you betray them or let them down, the payback will be extreme. You may never work in the same industry again.

Overall, however, the Taurus chief is a good chief. You'll know where you are with him or her; this sign is dependable to a fault, and you can trust the Bull's judgement. If you are hired by a Taurus – and they'll take their time reaching that decision – unless you are feckless, lazy, incompetent or disloyal, you can expect a long contract. Indeed, you should have a job for life and probably a lot of good food and wine to help ease those horns-locked moments.

THE TAURUS EMPLOYEE

Above all the Taurus employee seeks job security. Whether he or she is a construction worker, a recruitment officer, a bus driver or a financial advisor, top of the list of a Taurean's needs and expectations will be long-term employment.

When interviewing Mr or Ms Taurus, expect to be grilled (not literally, of course) albeit in a charming manner. Taureans need to know exactly what they're in for. Information about the business and their role in it should be clear, concise and without frills. It will be no use making such statements as: 'If you play your cards right, there could be a generous bonus at the end of the year.' If you're going to bring up the subject of a bonus, or any other tempting morsel, it had better be written into the contract.

Taureans don't do maybes.

While, as we have seen, Taurus produces some great singers and dancers, by and large this is a sign that gravitates to careers in business and the service industries: accountancy, insurance, hotel management, the building industry, catering and nursing – these are the Taurean realms. Sales and promotions are not their metier. Rather like themselves – they are what it says on the tin – they balk at the idea of sexing up a product for the sake of a sale. When they lie, their necks turn red and their noses get longer! (Only joking, although they will exhibit physical symptoms if forced to back anything they do not believe in.)

One of the great advantages of Taurean employees is that you can rely on them. They will arrive on time, leave on time and immediately put in for overtime if they've exceeded their hours. They like routines and will be happy to create routines for the rest of the staff, thereby increasing efficiency and productivity. When you give the celestial Bull an instruction, you can be sure it will be carried out; likewise, if you change anything in the brief, it will be brought to your attention.

Taurus likes a tight ship.

Think for a moment of the Wall Street Bull, that symbol of financial power. It was

chosen because the bull in nature is a powerful animal – aggressive, fixed of purpose and able to defend itself from attack. And in a similar vein the celestial Bull's power lies in his or her ability to stand strong in times of crisis. They are steadfast and forbearing. Plus, Taureans like money: they are good with money; and by the end of their working lives they will usually have accumulated enough funds and assets to carry them through to a very old age.

Think too about the way the bull in nature defends itself: cloven feet thrust firmly into the ground, head down and nostrils flaring. The instinct to block and resist is innate in all Taureans. Put an idea before them and their knee-jerk response is to reject it. However, this is more of a delaying tactic and, given enough time to think about the suggestion, they can come around. But it's a slow process.

Loyalty and trust are big issues for this Fixed earth sign. If a Taurean works for you, he (or she) is going to go to the mat for you, but if you let him down or fail to live up to your promises, he can become vengeful. An anonymous tip to the tax office suggesting irregularities in the company accounts would not be a bridge too far for a used-and-abused Taurean employee.

And speaking of crime, Taureans are rarely the fraudsters and villains of the zodiac; they are straight shooters and worthy of great trust. However, if you have employed a Taurean who's gone to the dark side, his or her crimes will be spectacular.

Taureans never do anything by halves.

Kindness is key. Beneath their reserved and conservative exteriors beat some of the kindest hearts in the zodiac. And although they might be difficult to budge on matters of protocol and principle they can be moved by a desperate plight, as long as it's not been self-administered. Taureans will help the weak, the suffering and the genuinely in need.

All in all, unless you expect speed, innovation and flexibility from your employee, you're going to be delighted with your Taurean member of staff. But watch your back: slow and steady wins the race and you may find your Taurean underling taking your place further down the line.

CAREERS FOR
MR OR MS
TAURUS

BEAUTY-BUSINESS
OWNER

CHEF/
CATERER

TEXTILE
MANUFACTURER

INVESTOR

PROPERTY
DEVELOPER/
ESTATE AGENT

BUILDER

ACCOUNTANT

FARMER/
GARDENER/
LANDSCAPE
GARDENER

INSURANCE
BROKER

NURSE

VIRGO IN THE WORKPLACE

23 AUGUST–21 SEPTEMBER

Element: Earth
Modality: Mutable
Ruling planet: Mercury

CURRICULUM VITAE

Virgo is the most adaptable and open-minded of the earth signs; a factor due to its Mutable[8] modality. The Mutables (Pisces, Gemini and Sagittarius are the others) like to keep their options open; they require a degree of freedom; they are concerned with the journey rather than the destination. In this way the element earth, usually rooted in the real and the rational, and highly resistant to change, acquires an airy dimension.

Virgo comes in at the beginning of autumn when the heat of the summer is dwindling and the winds are picking up, blowing the leaves off the trees. Which is why this sign is associated with gathering and distribution. To members of the sign, gathering and distributing do not refer to the harvesting of crops and the fruits of the earth, although Virgos are often advocates of organic produce and passionate about nature, but to Virgos' quest for knowledge and information and its dispersal.

STRENGTHS
Diligent
Industrious
Resourceful
Conscientious

WEAKNESSES
Hyper-critical
Argumentative
Defensive
Passive-aggressive

See modalities in the section on *How Astrology Works.*

To Virgo knowledge is all.

Virgo is ruled by Mercury – the planet of communication – so it should be no surprise to learn that many Virgos find their way into the teaching professions, academia and the communications industries. However, whereas Mercury-ruled Gemini can be an intellectual magpie and something of a lightweight, Virgo's thought processes and impulses are deep and complex.

Even if you know little else about astrology you are probably familiar with the notion that Virgos are the pernickety people of the zodiac; always ready to dot the Is and cross the Ts: they are devils for detail. However, they are not perfectionists per se: Virgos want to be the best they can be, they are meticulous; they seek excellence. And that's different from perfectionism.

Of all three earth signs, Virgo is the least ambitious. These individuals prefer to work behind the scenes; to be the power behind the throne. They hide behind masks, both to protect their vulnerable interior and to allow them to operate in secret. For this reason, many Virgos become actors, film directors and documentary makers. And there are plenty of them in the intelligence services.

Virgos are the craftsmen and the artisans of the zodiac. They love the authentic,

the natural and the worthwhile. They don't make a song and dance about themselves, but in every walk of life, every business, the individual keeping it all together, the one who knows where the bodies are buried and how much the company is worth to the last cent, will be a Virgo.

Underestimate them at your peril.

THE VIRGO BOSS

Bosses come in all shapes and sizes and all signs of the zodiac but, by and large, Virgo is not comfortable in the hot seat and much happier left of centre. He or she is not cut out to issue orders and arouse fear and dread in the staff. Virgos lead by example; they prefer a cooperative to a conglomerate. They keep things simple. Warren Buffett is an outstanding example of the Virgo CEO: still residing in the same Omaha house that he bought in 1958, his style of management has been described as 'hands off' and his advice to those following in his footsteps is 'Admit mistakes and stay humble.' Humility may be a Virgo attribute, but the ability to admit mistakes does not come easily to this sign. Virgos do everything to the absolute best of their ability; they are beyond criticism. Please understand this. If you're working for a Virgo boss, don't even think about pointing out an error in his or her thinking. Given time and more research – and Virgo bosses are a diligent bunch – they'll soon discover their own mistakes.

Warren Buffett: Sun and Neptune in Virgo.

Your Virgo boss will not employ you on your winning personality: your CV will be carefully dissected; references will be followed up and background checks performed. (You'd better not have embellished your employment history.) Then, and only then, will you be considered. You will be expected to live up to the company's high standards. These bosses have reached the top by painstaking effort and they'll

assume you will do the same. If you fail in your endeavours Mr or Ms Virgo won't shout and scream at you and hurl paperweights across the room: a pregnant silence before a small verbal jab delivered with precision to your jugular is more in style.

Virgos could give masterclasses in sarcasm and passive aggression.

Do not expect the Virgo boss to be a cheerleader either. Virgos believe their staff should be self-motivated enough to get the job done without constant encouragement and promises of rewards. The satisfaction of a job well done is enough for them and it should be enough for you, the employee, too.

Strangely enough, the office of your Virgo boss may not be as pin neat as his or her astrological CV would have you believe. Virgos know where everything is and they are very fond of labels and codes, but organized chaos is more often what you'll find. Don't make a comment, though. Make a note.

Virgos are natural-born caretakers. They flock like lemmings into the health and healing industries, the social services and human resources. But unlike their opposite number, the celestial Fish, Virgos do not mollycoddle. If you're in trouble the Virgo boss will listen carefully to your tale of woe, then point you in the direction of your salvation.

While Pisces will feed you fish, Virgos teach you how to fish.

Something you will not know from the appearance of your Virgo boss is that he or she is a dreadful worrier. Behind that *Mona Lisa* smile is a febrile imagination. Virgos are permanently tuned to the voice of their fears, which can get out of hand because they do not like to share their concerns. Top of the list of worries is invariably health. A small rash, an indefinable ache and a general feeling of malaise

will have them consulting Dr Google and realizing things are even worse than they thought. Always have a hand sanitizer on your person, some painkillers and tubes of fizzy vitamin C. Your boss will sense a kindred spirit. Your stock will rise.

The Virgo CEO will welcome ideas and suggestions (provided they cannot be interpreted as criticisms). This is a Mutable sign and the receiving and dispersing of information is as necessary as breathing. However, your boss will want any ideas backed up with evidence and accompanied by a detailed plan of action, which he or she can then nip and tuck and generally improve.

Your Virgo boss may not be the cuddliest creature on planet workplace nor the most adventurous and dynamic, but gradually, gradually you will come to respect his or her quiet, thoughtful ways. You will come to understand that while she (or he) is not constantly inquiring after your health and happiness, she *is* keeping a check on your well-being.

Virgo bosses may not share, but they care.

THE VIRGO EMPLOYEE

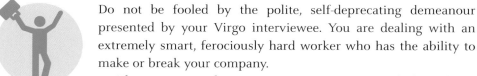

Do not be fooled by the polite, self-deprecating demeanour presented by your Virgo interviewee. You are dealing with an extremely smart, ferociously hard worker who has the ability to make or break your company.

The moment you hire a Virgo, you can rest easy in the knowledge that what you ask of him or her will be done, and on time and in triplicate! Members of this sign are dedicated, responsible and dutiful: they give their all to any task demanded of them. You don't have to ask them to put in overtime: they volunteer to work extra hours, and they'll make tea. They won't complain to you, but they will whinge to others.

There's something of the martyr in most Virgos.

Your Virgo employee is thoughtful and attentive. You only have to mention something once for it to be deposited in his or her extensive bank of knowledge, ready to be brought out when needed. Along with this ability to store information is the penchant for detail. It will be the Virgo working in the back room of a company who figures out that a penny saved on a weekly account could make the company millions over the years. And it will be the Virgo on the team who notices minute changes to a story that lead to the uncovering of a crime. If you're looking for an intelligence officer or a continuity person, find a Virgo.

These earthy Mercurials make excellent analysts and researchers. They love taking something apart and putting it back together piece by piece. In this way they get to the root of a problem. However, for the same reason sometimes they see only the trees and the wood is lost on them. Virgos do not always get the big picture. Nor are they naturals in the creative departments of organizations – leaps of faith and flashes of inspiration are not really their thing. (If you do have a wildly

inventive risk-taker Virgoan on your staff, there's almost certainly a strong Uranus-Jupiter theme in the natal chart.)

Virgos can work in a team, but they are better as soloists. While they enjoy spirited arguments and the exchange of ideas and information, they are not the touchy-feely/kumbaya people of the zodiac. They do not like their personal space being invaded; closeness is reserved for a chosen few. It is easy to see why Virgos are at home in libraries, museums and churches: silence is soothing and inspires contemplation.

Paradoxically, Virgos love to gossip. These are the people to head for if you want to know what's doing the rounds under the radar. They probably also know that research has proved the more intelligent you are, the more you love gossip... #super-smart!

One thing you need to get straight from the outset – your Virgo employee is beyond reproach and rarely, if ever, wrong. They are flawless: they cannot accept flaws in themselves and they certainly won't accept them in others. In the workplace

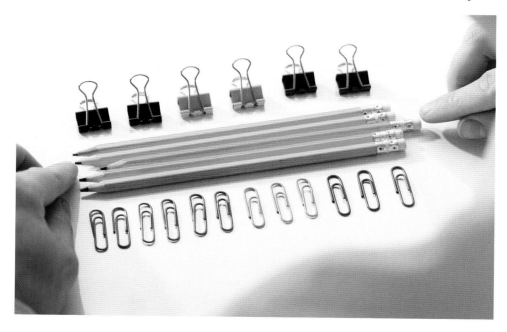

this attitude can create problems. Few people enjoy their faults being pointed out to them time after time. It makes for tension and ironically leads to a decline in production.

Another issue to bear in mind is that Virgos are not the most physically robust people, in large part because they worry a lot and keep their worries to themselves. In consequence, they can develop a variety of ailments, usually of a digestive and psychosomatic nature, which can lead to periodic absences from work. (Never seat them near the air-conditioning outlet.) They can also be allergy-prone, and if a member of staff suffers from EHS (electromagnetic hypersensitivity) when exposed to wi-fi stations, mobile phones and computer screens, you can bet there's Virgo somewhere in the chart.

However, these are small niggles about an otherwise stellar employee. Virgos are honourable, plain-speaking, helpful and efficient. You can forget about bells and whistles and riotous assemblies: these are the worker bees of the zodiac and worth their weight in golden honey.

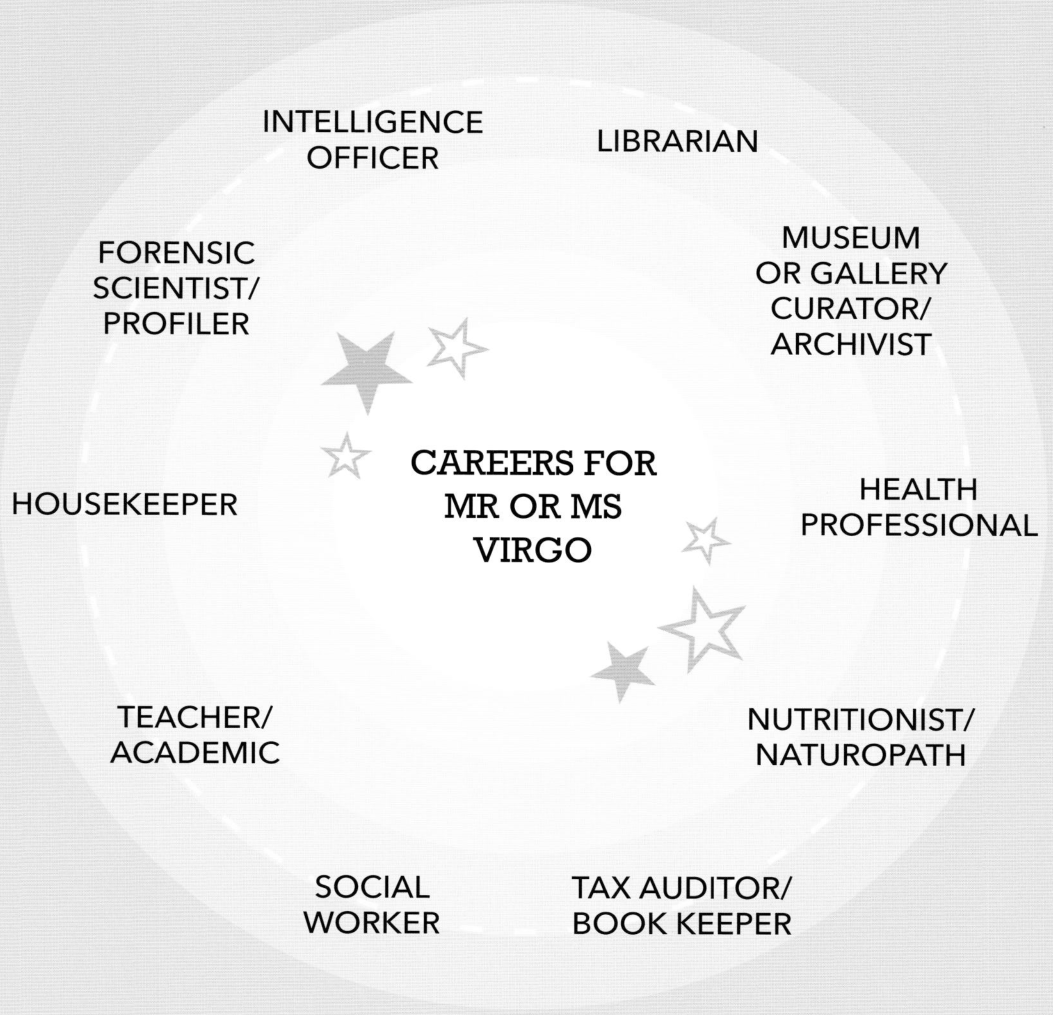

INTELLIGENCE OFFICER

LIBRARIAN

FORENSIC SCIENTIST/ PROFILER

MUSEUM OR GALLERY CURATOR/ ARCHIVIST

CAREERS FOR MR OR MS VIRGO

HOUSEKEEPER

HEALTH PROFESSIONAL

TEACHER/ ACADEMIC

NUTRITIONIST/ NATUROPATH

SOCIAL WORKER

TAX AUDITOR/ BOOK KEEPER

CAPRICORN IN THE WORKPLACE

21 DECEMBER–19 JANUARY

Element: Earth
Modality: Cardinal
Ruling planet: Saturn

CURRICULUM VITAE

The third and last of the earth signs epitomizes the strength, resilience and endurance of this element. In Capricorn the solidness of earth combines with the dynamism of its Cardinal modality[9]. Capricorn is the the architect of the zodiac; celestial Goats are the leaders and powerhouses among us.

The Sun enters the sign of Capricorn at the winter solstice. It is the season of long nights and short days, frosty mornings and bitterly cold nights. There are no leaves on the trees, no flowers in the fields: to all intents and purposes the earth is dead. Yet it is at this point in the year that the Earth begins its journey 'back to the sun'[10].

All the earth signs have an affinity with nature but it is Capricorn who relates most to the notion

> **STRENGTHS**
> Self-sufficient
> Patient
> Stable
> Constant
>
> **WEAKNESSES**
> Conceited
> Hidebound
> Dictatorial
> Uncompassionate

9   See modalities in the section on *How Astrology Works.*
10 As the Earth orbits the Sun, on or around 21 December the orientation of its tilt changes with respect to the position of the Sun.

that 'to every thing there is a season... a time to plant and a time to pluck up that which is planted'. The certain knowledge that all things come together in time is at once a spiritual and a rational statement, entirely in keeping with the symbol of the sign which is half goat and half fish: the reliable, hard-headed Goat has his tail in the sea of the unconscious mind and the waters of the spiritual and the divine.

Which is why it is no mere coincidence that we celebrate the birth of Jesus Christ in the time of Capricorn and that such historical figures as Joan of Arc and Nostradamus belong to this formidable earth sign.

The principle of time which is embedded in Capricorn owes much to its ruling planet, Saturn – the Lord of Time. This planet, once the remote outpost of the solar system and now the guardian of the gateway to the outer planets, resonates with the theme of boundaries and the passage of time.

Capricorn people do not believe in rushing into anything. They will research, contemplate and plan before they take action; they need to know what the outcome will be or at least the most likely result. They are great believers in tradition and value the lessons of the past. Unlike Taurus, they are not resistant to change, they understand that growth requires change, but that doesn't mean they'll embrace it immediately. And unlike Virgo, they can be fiercely ambitious.

There are, however, two kinds of Goats: those who prefer the lower pastures, enjoying the routine of life, doing the job they were born to do; and those who crave the pinnacles of power, for whom no terrain is too formidable, no obstacle unsurmountable, on their journey to the top. One thing they both share, however, is an ability to withstand any amount of aggravation and opposition. No matter how long it takes they'll get there in the end.

All things come together in time for Capricorn.

THE CAPRICORN BOSS

 No matter how small in physical stature your Capricorn boss may be, he or she exudes power and strength. Capricorn chiefs command respect; you instinctively know not to mess with them.

The first thing you must realize about your Saturnian boss is that it has taken this person a long time to get the top job, and along the way they've overcome more hurdles than you've had hot dinners: if life were the Olympic Games, Capricorn would be competing in the triathlon. And winning. And in the same way that your boss pits himself against the elements on a regular basis you will only gain his or her respect and permanent employment if you show the same grit and determination. Indeed, the celestial Goat sets more store by consistent, conscientious hard work than by results. Of course, Capricorns want results, but because they appreciate the importance of time, if they can see potential in an employee they will wait patiently until that promise is fulfilled.

The Saturnian boss also understands the value of working your way up from the first rung of the company ladder. Even a Capricorn entering the family firm will expect to start at the bottom and rise through the ranks. And speaking of family, there is something of the patriarch or matriarch in Capricorns: they believe in dynasties, whether they recognize they have a duty to preserve the bloodline, grow the family business or found their own corporate empire. And like all good parents, they nurture their young; they believe in order and discipline; they will be firm but fair.

Then again, the notion that power corrupts and absolute power corrupts absolutely is something all Capricorns need to bear in mind. Kim Jong-un belongs to team Capricorn, as did Chairman Mao and Richard Nixon.

Status is important to this Saturn-ruled boss. He or she not only appreciates the trappings of high position, but also enjoys hobnobbing and being associated with other people of power and influence. Aside from revealing your supreme work ethic to your Capricorn boss, if you can drop a few important names in your interview, that's going to help.

Of all the things anathema to Capricorn, losing face comes near the top of the list. Never do anything that could embarrass this boss. An ill-chosen remark at a board meeting, a sudden loss of composure in public, or a little too much alcohol-driven revelry at the Christmas party could put your job in jeopardy. The celestial Goat sets great store by his (or her) image: he tends to be the class act of the zodiac and does

not appreciate loose or louche behaviour.

Capricorns take to leadership at an early age. If you're watching children at play, the one calling the shots, the one the others appear to be following, is sure to have some Capricorn in the chart. Saturn-ruled bosses do not simply crave control because they relish the sense of power, but because they believe no one can do the job as well as they can. Yes, they'll delegate responsibility,

but a constant eye will be kept on that employee to ensure nothing goes wrong.

Capricorns are the puppet masters of the zodiac.

The Saturnians may believe in dynasties but that does not necessarily mean they have a lot of time for them in the sense of actually being there. This sign breeds workaholics and celestial Goats tend to spend more time in the office than they do at home. While this creates problems in their private lives it also means that they are not always sympathetic to their staff when problems and demands of family life require support and time off.

When you sign a Capricorn contract your loyalties are to the company.

Sometimes you may find your Capricorn boss difficult to reach. He or she may be sitting in front of you, but you can't seem to make a connection. On many occasions this is because they have a matter that is greatly bothering them, and the more they focus on it, the darker and bleaker and more distant they become. You will have to get used to Mr or Ms Goat disappearing down a black hole. They will surface eventually, but don't try to edge them out before they're ready. Once they've got a solution, and only when they've got a solution, will they emerge.

Like the sure-footed goat in nature, Capricorn is a steady, steadfast, stalwart boss. When things get tough, the celestial Goat raises her (or his) game, gathers the troops together and turns the situation around. You can trust this boss to meet her obligations, which, of course, include you, and to be at the helm of her ship day and night, if necessary. In return the Saturnian will expect commitment and consistency from you.

Fluff and flummery, junkets and jamborees have no place in a Capricorn workplace; hard work, long hours and dedication to the company cause do.

THE CAPRICORN EMPLOYEE

 Before you think of signing on a Capricorn employee, bear in mind that he (or she) has set his sights on your job, or maybe one even better. These are the rock climbers of the professional world and within every Capricorn lies a heart pumping with ambition. Far from this knowledge deterring you, it should inspire you immediately to hand them a contract.

You will not find a more responsible, hard-working, thorough and astute individual.

Mr and Ms Goat are looking for a job with prospects. They are prepared to start at the bottom and climb to the top, but they will want assurances that promotion based on results is part of the package. They will also require a pension and a key to the executive rest room. (That's an exaggeration, of course, but if they could have some trappings of high office, they would be delighted. They would work even harder.)

Looking around the workplace you'll be able to spot the celestial Goat. She (or he) won't be the one regaling colleagues with accounts of wild nights and past conquests – Capricorn may be one of the hornier members of the zodiac, but only in private – and she won't be the one shouting abuse down the telephone. Nor will Capricorn be the one in the low-cut shirt and the thigh-high skirt. No, the office Saturnian will be quietly getting on with work, taking in all the indiscretions and noting any slipshod practices just in case such information could come in handy at a future date.

And you will rarely find the Capricorn employee fraternizing during working hours with colleagues, and never at all with subordinates. These individuals understand the benefit of being seen with the right people in the right places.

Status is far more important than popularity.

And while we're on the subject of status and position, Capricorns tend to marry where they want to go. If you're going to fall in love and marry, why shouldn't it be the boss or the boss's offspring? Whether Capricorn is an employee of a bank, an insurance company or the government (all three of which have Capricorn written all over them) they will diligently deal with the task in hand while keeping an eye on a more rewarding opportunity. They will put themselves forward for challenging projects that provide kudos, although their more usual tactic is to find a sponsor to recommend them.

Members of this sign are not beyond manipulation and opportunism.

One of their greatest assets is their ability to solve problems. Like everything else in life, they start at the beginning and work their way through until they've found a solution. They are able to leave emotions out of the mix, which allows

them to focus on the realities and the practicalities of the problem. They are superb strategists and excellent decision-makers.

Capricorns never dither; they're doers.

On the down side, your Capricorn employee may not be the most innovative and creative member of the team. And he or she does have a tendency to pour cold water over the ideas of those who do. This behaviour

is not a form of envy but a result of a kind of terminal caution. The way to handle the Saturnian stonewaller is to give him or her the task of establishing whether or not an idea is workable. That way Mr or Ms Goat gets some kudos if it proves successful.

Another little issue with the Capricorn employee is that he or she can be very slow. If you want a job done quickly, don't ask the Goat. Not only does Capricorn take its time ensuring that all the facts and figures are correct, but she (or he) tends to spend rather too long getting everything in order before she even begins. The threat of a deadline can sometimes completely paralyse her. In part this has to do with a Capricorn's fear that she (or he) might not be able to deliver the results she expect of herself. There's little point putting any pressure on her to complete a task: when it's done it's done, and it will be perfect.

Capricorns are high achievers.

This sign is usually good with money, which is the reason financial institutions are chock-full of Capricorns. However, the combination of their talent for figures and their need for boundaries can make them not just frugal but downright stingy. These won't be the staff members popping handfuls of cash into the pot for a leaving present or the company do.

If you're looking for an employee who will lighten your day and lift your spirit, Capricorn is not going to be your first choice. However, if you want someone who will lighten your load, someone for whom no burden is too heavy, no task too great; someone who can wear the mantle of responsibility, and be there in those tough moments, Mr and Ms Goat are your people.

CIVIL SERVANT

BANKER

LEGISLATOR

MILITARY OFFICER

SURVEYOR

CAREERS FOR MR OR MS CAPRICORN

POLICE OFFICER

ARCHITECT

JUDGE/ MAGISTRATE

DENTIST

INTERNAL REVENUE INSPECTOR

INTER-RELATIONSHIPS
Who gets on with whom
in the workplace

EARTH-EARTH

Atlas Securities, founded in 1679, proprietors: C. A. Bull and B. Ware-Goat.

Of course, this is a fictitious company, but it is the perfect example of what an earth/earth business might be. Two earth signs come from the same place and are going to the same place, and with steady, determined, persistent footsteps. Earth signs require things to last and to prove reliable and consistent over the years. Earth/earth businesses are made of the right stuff.

In the workplace two earth signs work well together. They operate at the same tempo and see situations in a similar way. They're not going to get hysterical over a bit of bad publicity or news that the market value of the company is falling. Time and effort will overcome all problems.

Earth signs have a mutual respect for each other's methods; they will support one another; they will work things out, even if they don't actually like each other. And they will always unite to oppose colleagues who want to move too fast or display a reckless disregard for safety, solvency, history and company policy.

A scandalous romance is not something you'd expect from two earth signs in the workplace. If there is an attraction between them, either they'll ignore it or one of them will leave.

The downside to earth–earth combinations is that they are a formidable blocking act. Too much earth, and steady progress might be closer to dead slow and stop. A little earth, and you'll have a team that will get you to the top of the mountain, safe and sure.

And the mix of earth signs makes a difference too. Same signs usually get on extremely well: it all depends whether the mirror image is positive or negative. Virgo's thoroughness ensures Capricorn's grand plans will not fail because of a missed step and Virgo helps Taurus to open his or her mind to alternatives. Taurus works with Capricorn to ride over all bumps in the road and get there in the end, and under budget. And Taurus provides a solid shoulder to lean on when Virgo's anxieties and pedantry get in the way of office harmony and the completion of a project. Last but not least, Capricorn manages to season Virgo's excellent work ethic with a little ambition and the Goat is one of the only signs able to budge Taurus when those toes are well and truly dug in.

All in all, earth signs guarantee the company ship travels safely and surely across all seas in all weathers.

EARTH-FIRE

Earth and fire are not an easy mix. Fire scorches earth, while earth puts out fire. These two groups have totally different agendas, totally different personalities. This does not mean, however, that they have nothing to offer one another in the workplace: it's just going to be a bumpy ride.

Taurus, Virgo and Capricorn require considerable time to think through a project and mount a strategy while Aries, Leo and Sagittarius like to get on with the job as soon as possible, flying by the seat of their pants. Thus, earth becomes exasperated by fire while fire gets enormously frustrated with earth.

The earth signs also tend to view their fiery colleagues and superiors as slightly superficial and childish while Aries, Leo and Sagittarius perceive the earth signs as rather a dull crew.

However, there are advantages to earth/fire workplaces. Indeed, there is a name

for this sun-sign combination – the steamroller. Fire's irresistible force and optimism and earth's tenacity, strategy and realism make for an extremely powerful working relationship. They just won't want to go off to the same pub after work.

The dynamic between earth and fire is especially potent when they share a modality. An earth/fire relationship involving Capricorn and Aries, Taurus and Leo and Virgo and

Sagittarius characterize the best and worst of the steamroller. The reason being that although they operate at different speeds and with contrasting mechanisms, they have a core connection. And that core connection is their shared modality. Sharing a modality is akin to belonging to the same family, but, like a family, they may not always function well as a unit. Sun signs that are 90 degrees away from each other have a dysfunctional relationship.

Horns tend to get locked rather too frequently when Aries and Taurus work together and Virgos just irritate the hell out of Aries with their pernickety ways. Leo and Capricorn can have a positive dynamic but it's similar to having two alpha males on a team; and constant bickering between Leo and Virgo interferes with office harmony and progress. Sagittarius and Capricorn do not view the world through the same lens: they rarely agree on anything; as for an Archer and a Bull – it's a case of the irresistible force meeting the immoveable object.

The secret to working well together, whatever the earth/fire sign mix, is that fiery people need to appreciate the value of caution and foresight and must cease to expect their earthy colleagues to deal with all the humdrum aspects of business. Earthy people, on the other hand, must acknowledge the importance of seizing the

moment and recognize where they are unnecessarily using blocking and delaying tactics.

EARTH-WATER

Water nourishes earth, enabling it to become fruitful, while earth holds water and prevents it from running all over the place. Both the fire signs and the water signs bring creativity and inspiration into the workplace, but while Aries, Leo and Sagittarius run rampant over earth's need for structure, discipline and caution, Cancer, Scorpio and Pisces encourage the earth signs to go beyond the boundaries of their imagination. They bring out the best in them.

Earth's stability and dependability is a perfect foil for water's insecurity and vulnerability. The earth signs rarely feel hot and bothered as they do in fire's company nor ruffled and confused as in air's vicinity. Water responds instinctively and undemandingly to earth while earth to them represents strength and steadfastness.

The exchange between earth and water signs is pleasant and rewarding. There's a nice little hum in the office. They like to sit near each other and hang out together at the coffee station. Cancer, Scorpio and Pisces are not the types to insist on their own way at all costs, although Scorpio can be bloody-minded at times, and they welcome Capricorn's leadership, Taurus's commitment and Virgo's pragmatism.

The best earth/water combinations are those that involve signs that are 60 degrees apart: this is an angle of harmony and positive diversity. This is why Taurus's best workmates are Cancer and Pisces; Virgo's are Cancer and Scorpio and Capricorn's are Scorpio and Pisces.

Virgo is Pisces' opposite number in the zodiac and both belong to the Mutable family, so they share certain preferences, behaviours and each other's vices and virtues. Virgo and Pisces can go round and round in circles, sometimes losing the end game completely, and they both have passive-aggressive tendencies, but when they work well together, they're a brilliant team. They will, incidentally, be the supplier of pills and potions to the office population and the members of staff guaranteed to know the source of your sore thumb.

Capricorn is Cancer's polar opposite, and there is a mutual give and take to this working relationship. Taurus and Scorpio, by contrast, tend to bring out one another's worst points, although if there is one team guaranteed to go down with the ship it's going to be this one.

If there is a problem with an earth/water relationship it lies in their both being too cautious and pessimistic. While the earth signs maintain they're only being realistic, water signs cannot explain their reservations: they just *feel* something is not going to work, and they just *know* in their bones they're right. Thus, as a working couple they compound their mutual negativity, and this can slow down progress and ruin the normally warm and cooperative atmosphere.

But, by and large, earth signs and water signs make a great team.

EARTH-AIR

Air may play an essential role in transporting the seeds that make earth fruitful, but winds and breezes stir up plenty of dust. Consequently, earth/air combinations can be fractious in the workplace, although not half as awkward as in romantic and sexual relationships.

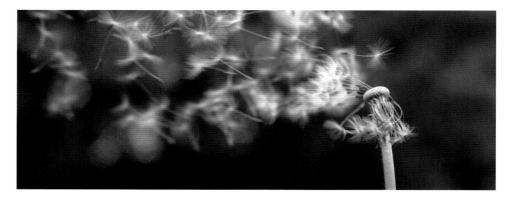

The earth signs find Gemini, Libra and Aquarius a tad lightweight and far too charming for their own good. They may even describe them as empty shells. Air signs, on the other hand, tend to feel stifled by earth's slow and conservative manner. They sometimes refer to them as troglodytes. Fortunately, neither element group allows emotion to overcome reason, so while a hard frost may descend on boardroom meetings from time to time, they'll usually find consensus, even if it is only to agree to disagree.

One of the reasons that earth and air make sense in the workplace is that they are ruled by the same planets: Saturn rules both Capricorn and Aquarius; Venus rules both Taurus and Libra and Mercury rules both Virgo and Gemini. And a shared rulership makes for an innate understanding of and respect for each other's standpoint. Capricorn and Aquarius understand the need for structure; Taurus and Libra share a need for harmony and form while Virgo and Gemini are natural disseminators – to both, knowledge and information is the very stuff of life.

Where an earth sign shares a modality with an air sign, there is a common bond, so Capricorn and Libra, Taurus and Aquarius and Virgo and Gemini represent the best of the air/earth combinations, although when this working relationship goes sour it can become irreversible. Someone has to go.

Earth, as we know, is intensely practical; air is theoretical, but in business this can work. Those earthy seeds that air can disperse mean that some of earth's brilliant ideas that might otherwise never get off the ground actually find a home.

Another plus to this pairing's mutual disregard for emotions in business is that finances do not scare them. Money is money; it's a commodity. In investment houses and merchant banks across the globe air and earth signs keep a cool head and a firm grasp on the tiller when markets collapse and currencies are devalued.

Despite their very different natures, there is some fertile common ground between air and earth signs. They may even be the best of the combinations in the workplace.

STAR RATING BETWEEN TAURUS, VIRGO AND CAPRICORN AND THE REST OF THE ZODIAC

	TAURUS	VIRGO	CAPRICORN
ARIES	★	★	★
TAURUS	★ ★ ★ ★	★ ★ ★ ★	★ ★ ★ ★
GEMINI	★	★ ★ ★	★ ★
CANCER	★ ★ ★ ★ ★	★ ★ ★ ★ ★	★ ★ ★ ★
LEO	★	★	★
VIRGO	★ ★ ★ ★	★ ★ ★ ★	★ ★ ★ ★
LIBRA	★ ★ ★	★	★ ★
SCORPIO	★ ★	★ ★ ★ ★ ★	★ ★ ★ ★ ★
SAGITTARIUS	★	★	★
CAPRICORN	★ ★ ★ ★	★ ★ ★ ★	★ ★ ★ ★
AQUARIUS	★ ★	★	★ ★ ★
PISCES	★ ★ ★ ★ ★	★ ★ ★	★ ★ ★ ★ ★

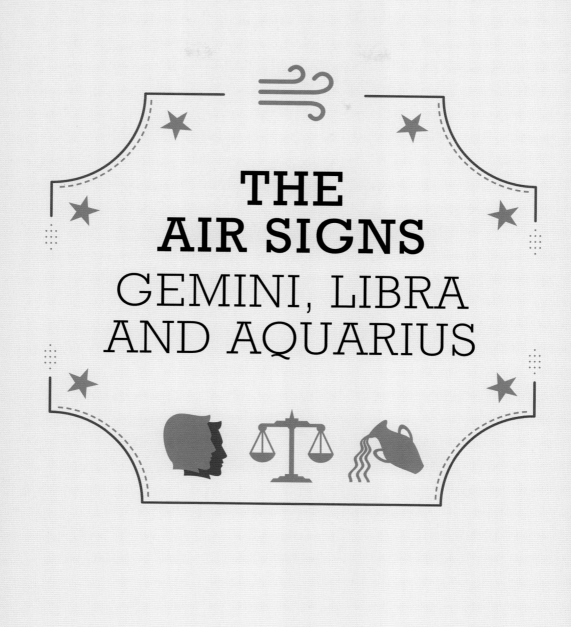

THE
AIR SIGNS
GEMINI, LIBRA AND AQUARIUS

THE ELEMENT AIR

Every living being breathes air; without it, we would cease to exist. Such a statement might give rise to the notion that air is the most important of the elements, but no element is greater than another: they are simply four basic principles of life, which, when applied to personality, describe four essential types. Fire is creative and spontaneous, earth is practical and solid, water is emotional and imaginative, and air is cerebral and detached.

Air is all about us, yet we cannot see it or touch it: we feel it when light breezes brush across our bodies or we get blown off our feet in a force-ten gale. Air is synonymous with *prana*, the term yogis use to describe the breath of life. The element air belongs to the realm of thoughts and concepts. Air disperses seeds which fall to earth, and, watered by the rains and warmed by the sun, grow into plants.

The air signs seed ideas and wait for others to bring them into reality.

While the majority of zodiac signs are represented by animals, Gemini is

symbolized by the celestial twins, Libra a pair of scales and Aquarius a man bearing an urn, not full of water, by the way, but ether. These symbols reveal the air signs' roles as information gatherers and providers and impartial observers: these symbols also serve to remind us that it is our human consciousness that separates us from the animals.

Of all the remaining signs of the zodiac only Virgo is represented in human form, and this is the only other sign of the zodiac associated with thought and neutrality. And Virgo shares its ruler, Mercury, the planet of communication, with airy Gemini.

To the air signs knowledge and communication are as essential to life as breathing.

Gemini, Libra and Aquarius are sociable, logical and rational. They are able to separate emotions from reason, which is why you find so many of them in the legal profession, the teaching industry and academia and journalism.

Air signs do not enjoy being plunged into the waters of deep emotion: they may write epic love poems and make brilliant agony aunts, but they'd rather not subject themselves to raw intimacy. It's a little scary for them.

In Jungian psychology, which has much to offer astrology, of the four basic types the 'thinking' function is akin to the air element. 'Thinking' types respond to life through the intellect; they connect ideas in order to reach conclusions about what is going on in their world. And, as we shall see in the section on inter-relationships, 'thinking' (air) and 'intuition' (fire) are on the same spectrum as 'sensation' (earth) and 'feeling' (water).

Air signs are better at analysing their feelings than relating to them. Libra, although

a sign embodying the principle of relating, is nonetheless more concerned with the balance of a relationship and the fair and just behaviour of those participating. Librans are always ready to talk the talk but a little sketchy about walking the walk. Aquarius, while being concerned with humanity as a whole, can become utterly floored when required to deal with someone on a one-to-one emotional basis. As for Gemini, signing up to anything or anyone for life scares the pants off them. They can think themselves into and out of a relationship in the time it takes to say 'commitment-phobia'.

Air signs do not like to be contained, whether in the sense of boxing themselves into an intellectual corner or being confined to small spaces. They need room to manoeuvre. As a result of this open-ended attitude it can be enormously frustrating trying to establish what an air sign truly thinks. Aquarius is the exception here, given that this sign can be very opinionated and attached to its beliefs. Still, as with Gemini, Aquarians do not like people being able to read them and prefer a degree of invisibility.

Head over heart is the air-sign way. Emotional appeals have no impact on their judgement, which makes them brilliant negotiators. In a team, air signs are invaluable when trying to get everyone on the same page and defusing any upsets. If you need a mediator, call in an air sign. The downside to this quality of detachment is that the air signs can come across as cold and unfeeling.

Inasmuch as air can cool the temperature and calm stormy seas, it can also stir things up and get everyone rattled. These are the great debaters of the zodiac: they have an argument and an explanation for everything, so trying to get the better of Gemini, Libra and Aquarius in a dispute is at best an uphill struggle and worst, pointless. In fact, they rather enjoy generating controversy.

Air signs see the full picture and all the component parts. They can break down a project, a plan and a relationship into small pieces while maintaining its integrity. Air signs are thus a vital commodity in any workplace; it matters not whether they're in the recruitment business, in the aerospace industry, publishing, politics or travel (all air sign fields).

Without air we cannot breathe and without air signs we would never reach the stars.

There are degrees of airiness, though, and whether you are an air head with a genius for social media or an egghead with a mission to take us to Betelgeuse and beyond, depends on how many planets and points you have in air signs besides the Sun in your birth chart.

AIR ON A SCALE OF 1-10

If you are curious to know just how airy you or your boss, colleague or employee are, you'll need a birth date and, ideally, also a time and place of birth. Whether you use an online service to tabulate the chart for you or you yourself have the knowledge, establishing the degree of cool is easy: add up all the planets and points in air signs, according to the list below. It's simply a numbers game.

Ascendant = 3	Venus = 3	Saturn = 2
Sun = 3	Mars = 3	Uranus = 1
Moon = 3	Mid-heaven = 1	Neptune = 1
Mercury = 3	Jupiter = 2	Pluto = 1

If you score 9 points or more in air signs, you are liquid nitrogen in a bottle; between 5 and 8 you are chilled but not frozen; and between 1 and 4 you are cool to the touch and refreshing on the palate. People with a surfeit of air can be geniuses yet like all uber-cerebral individuals they are poor at picking up emotional signals. And responding to unspoken messages is as important in the workplace as it is in life. Explaining to a super airy person that you have a feeling about something will get you absolutely nowhere.

Tony Blair is a perfect example of the super airy individual: a total of 12 points in air, and although his Sun is in Taurus, which gives him a grounding in reality, the combination of his Ascendant and Mars in Gemini and Moon in Aquarius contribute to his epithet: The Great Communicator. Boris Johnson is yet another politician with a surfeit of air – 15 points in all including the Sun in Gemini: he is undeniably brilliant as both a writer and orator, although there is an aura of the mad scientist about him!

Indeed, air signs find a natural home in politics. Representing team Aquarius, we have Abraham Lincoln (Sun and Ascendant in Aquarius and Mars in Libra); Ronald Reagan (Sun Aquarius and Mid-heaven in Libra); Oprah Winfrey (Sun, Venus and Mercury in Aquarius); and Ayn Rand (Sun and Saturn in Aquarius). And Aquarius has more than its fair share of scientists and inventors too – Thomas Edison, Charles Darwin and Galileo to name but three.

As for the Libra clan: Mahatma Gandhi (Sun Libra), Margaret Thatcher (Sun,

Former British Prime Minister Tony Blair: 12 points in air.

Oprah Winfrey: 9 points in air.

Mercury and Mars in Libra), Theresa May (Sun Libra), David Cameron (Sun and Venus in Libra), Benjamin Netanyahu (Sun, Moon, Mercury and Neptune in Libra) and Vladimir Putin (Sun, Saturn, Mercury and Neptune in Libra and Moon in Gemini).

But, of course, the hall of fame also includes some names who have gone to the dark side – Heinrich Himmler (Libra), Aleister Crowley (Libra), Grigori Rasputin (Aquarius), and Aung San Suu Kyi (Gemini).

GEMINI IN THE WORKPLACE

21 MAY–21 JUNE

Element: Air
Modality: Mutable
Ruling planet: Mercury

CURRICULUM VITAE

A typical Gemini CV would run to several pages. Geminis love variety and change, and their job experience is eclectic to say the least. Some might describe them as jacks of all trades, masters of none. They are adaptable and quick-thinking and can turn their hands, or rather their minds, to anything they choose.

Gemini is the first of the air signs, beginning in late May and ending in late June. And there is indeed a spring-like quality to this sign. They are the Peter Pans of the zodiac, enduringly youthful, endlessly curious and disinclined to stick to a course unless it continues to engage them.

Ruled by Mercury, communication is Gemini's keyword, which makes members of this sign perfect for jobs that involve travel, movement, discussion, debate, research and speculation. You'll find clutches of Geminis in the worlds of finance, marketing, PR, IT, broadcasting and journalism; they thrive in careers that require they keep current and offer ever-expanding horizons.

STRENGTHS
Adaptable
Logical
Open-minded
Impartial

WEAKNESSES
Commitment-phobic
Evasive
Devious
Aloof

Geminis often suffer from FOMO (Fear Of Missing Out).

Gemini is the purest form of air, the reason being it is a Mutable[11] sign and the Mutables are equivocal and like to go with the flow: containment of any form – intellectual, physical or emotional – is anathema to them.

Of all the air signs, Gemini is the least ambitious. It is more important for Geminis to have options than to limit themselves to a specific goal, and being on a conveyor belt to the top is not their concept of what life should be. Geminis work to live, not the other way around. That Geminis are usually highly successful is due to their youthful enthusiasm and curiosity, their ingenuity and their refusal to be bound by what has gone before.

Gemini is far from all sweetness and light, however. In myth, Mercury was chosen for his stealth and cunning to ferry the souls of the dead to the underworld, and there is a dark interior to this sign that can emerge in some very unpleasant ways. The written and spoken word is a lethal weapon in Gemini hands.

The parts of the body ruled by Gemini are the lungs, the nervous system and the hands and arms. You can spot the Geminis in the workplace because they will be the ones waving their arms while talking to a captive audience. A smoke-free environment with plenty of light and air is essential for their physical and psychological well-being.

Never block the airflow.

---

11   Mutable signs are Gemini, Virgo, Sagittarius and Pisces: see the Introduction: How Astrology Works.

THE GEMINI BOSS

Meeting your Gemini boss for the first time is deceptively pleasant. Mr and Ms Gemini are informal, friendly, inquisitive and charming. Be taken in by this at your peril. Hidden among the anecdotes and amusing comments will be killer questions aimed at getting you to reveal aspects of yourself and your history you'd prefer to keep under wraps.

Come prepared for your interview not only with every part of the job and the company covered, but au fait with current affairs, what's trending on social media, who and what's in and out. And, as your masterstroke, deliver a humorous account of your recent stay in the ice hotel/your trip across the northern Atlantic on a container ship and how much you're enjoying learning Mandarin.

Geminis are brilliant conversationalists. They are open to new ideas and mould-breaking concepts. He or she will actively encourage open dialogue between employees and superiors, although in most Gemini-run establishments you'd be hard pressed to know who was who.

Hierarchies are not to a Mercurial's taste.

The Gemini boss is fond of holding informal weekly meetings to discuss issues and air problems, and there may be a box in which complaints can be placed, guaranteeing their author anonymity. But if you do make a written protest, be sure

it is well crafted with a pithy comment or two. The Gemini CEO goes to forensic lengths to discover the source of any grievance. Your witty, literary style could save your job.

A Gemini CEO is not a hands-on individual. Actually, this has a double meaning in that Geminis can be germ-phobic, as is Gemini Donald Trump, so getting up close and personal is to be avoided at all costs and, on the other hand, a Gemini boss will outline ideas and tasks and expect everyone else to get on with them while he or she is out and about making connections or behind closed doors wheeler-dealering.

And in keeping with Gemini's penchant for invisibility, his or her office may well have one-way vision glass. No one can see in, but the Gemini chief can see out.

Given that Geminis are an articulate bunch it is curious how many of them mumble. However, this is a strategy. Since these are the idea-seeders of the zodiac, they do not always know quite what it is they are striving to bring into being. So, they may utter a few vague instructions and a stream of endless sentences, and with a few hand waves and 'talk-to-you-laters' they've left the building.

Members of this sign may be brilliant multi-taskers yet their tendency to change their minds is confusing for those who must carry out their instructions. And don't expect your Gemini boss to take responsibility for any failures – remember Peter Pan. The finger of blame will be deftly pointed elsewhere. On the other hand, there is little that Geminis cannot turn around in the face of a disaster: their ingenuity is breathtaking.

Being bosses and growing companies does not render Geminis immune to the perennial problem of boredom. As long as other people are handling the responsibility of getting the job done, all is well, but should they have to be involved with the menial, mundane aspects of a project, they will become very fidgety and cranky. It's best not to try to jolly them out of their ill humour either – it is, after all, only temporary – because you are likely to be subjected to a barrage of sarcasm and become the focus of some very pointed remarks.

Normally, of course, your Gemini boss is the soul of good humour and full of ideas as to how to brighten up the dull office day. There'll be team outings, team activities and social intercourse will be encouraged by any and every means. You

may also have to field the occasional prank. This sign loves putting people on the spot and playing with their minds, so if, as an employee, you enter the building one day to find your office has disappeared – there is a blank wall where its door used to be – don't show offence: your quicksilver boss had it removed and plaster-boarded over, just for the hell of it! And in the Gemini boss's defence, should he or she be the object of a practical joke, it will all be taken in good part.

The Gemini boss may not be to everyone's taste – consistency, constancy, caution, stability and convention won't be part of the package – however, no one day will be like another, and if you can work under someone who is non-judgemental, ready to hear you out and encourage you to stretch the boundaries of your imagination, if not a lot more besides, make a beeline for the offices of the celestial Twin.

THE GEMINI EMPLOYEE

'We are looking for a bright, versatile sales executive to take on a cross-platform media sales role embracing digital streaming, publishing, events and awards.' This job is custom made for the archetypal Gemini. And, if the company advertising the position is smart, it will add: 'Having the Sun in Gemini could be an advantage.'

The Gemini seated before you in the candidate's chair will not necessarily be the person who shows up on the first day of work. This is because Geminis are the chameleons of the zodiac; their appearance, their opinions, their desires and interests resemble the Great British weather – all four seasons in one day. You may even request another look at their CV and your notes on the interview. Is this really the same person?

The only aspect of Gemini to be unchangeable and unchanging is its inconstant nature.

The interview is a preview, by the way, of what will follow should you employ Mr or Ms Gemini. In a short space of time the roles will have been reversed and for some inexplicable reason the Gemini candidate now appears to be interviewing you. You'll feel put on the spot when you cannot summon up the name of the Turkish foreign minister or the latest scientific research that found plants in the office reduce staff stress levels and a short walk before lunch increases the desire for fruit and vegetables. Oh, and where does everyone keep their in-house scooters?

Mr or Ms Gemini's main concern about the job will be how much freedom they will have to develop new products and strategies; how much freedom they will have, full stop. They require autonomy and to come and go as they please. Some days they'll work eight hours at a stretch and others they'll appear and disappear like the Cheshire Cat. Generous holiday time will be a plus, not necessarily paid either – just as long as they can get away at intervals during the working year. And they also prefer flexitime and short-term contracts. Your payback is an employee with an original mind who'll keep colleagues, seniors and juniors alike amused and on their toes, and you way ahead of the competition.

And the downside? Well, for every Dr Jekyll there is a Mr Hyde and some Geminis cannot altogether supress their dark twin: he or she often emerges in the tendency to cut their fellow workers down to size, burst their balloons and psychologically bully them. A trait shared by some Gemini bosses too. And, of course, because they are so artful with their derogation it is difficult for their victims to challenge them or to bring their behaviour to the attention of superiors.

Geminis have restless spirits and agile minds with the result that they can become bored with projects before they are completed, and should the job continue to fail to provide the stimulation they require, they will leave, sometimes at short notice and with very little guilt about dropping you in the soup.

This same agility and edginess, however, enables them to adapt with ease to changing circumstances. They rarely sulk or flap when faced with unexpected detours and derailments. This does not mean, however, that they will forget the inconvenience. Facts and trivia are not the only things that get deposited for future reference in the Gemini bank of knowledge and information.

Geminis' conversational skills and their ability to mirror other people (often completely unconscious) make them natural salesmen. Most of them could sell ice to Eskimos and certainly skin-firming potions to 20-somethings. And, of course, they could sell their client's innocence to a jury and persuade countless numbers that global warming is nonsense. And even when, ultimately, the Eskimos realize they've been played and the seas take over the land, somehow it's not Gemini's fault. He or she had presented you with the evidence and you made your decision.

In the same way that Geminis can convince you white is the new black, the line between good and evil can be easily crossed: it all depends what your meaning of a line is... To some, that ingenious money-making scheme is a new way forward, to others it looks suspiciously like fraud. So, when your Gemini employee presents you with an idea that could be said to be sailing close to the wind, don't get talked into it. Call in the Capricorns to check it out.

As we discovered earlier, Gemini is more concerned with autonomy and

freedom than whether paid holidays are part of the package, but this does not mean they don't care about making money. Gemini is one of the most financially savvy signs of the zodiac. Even if you have no intention of raising your Gemini employee's salary, by the time he or she has discussed the matter with you, you will be agreeing to the increase, and it will all seem so very, very logical.

Every workplace needs a Gemini employee. That's if you hope to keep pace with the competition, if not outstrip it. This employee will bring innovation, humour and diversity into the workplace. He (or she) will be worth his weight in mercury.

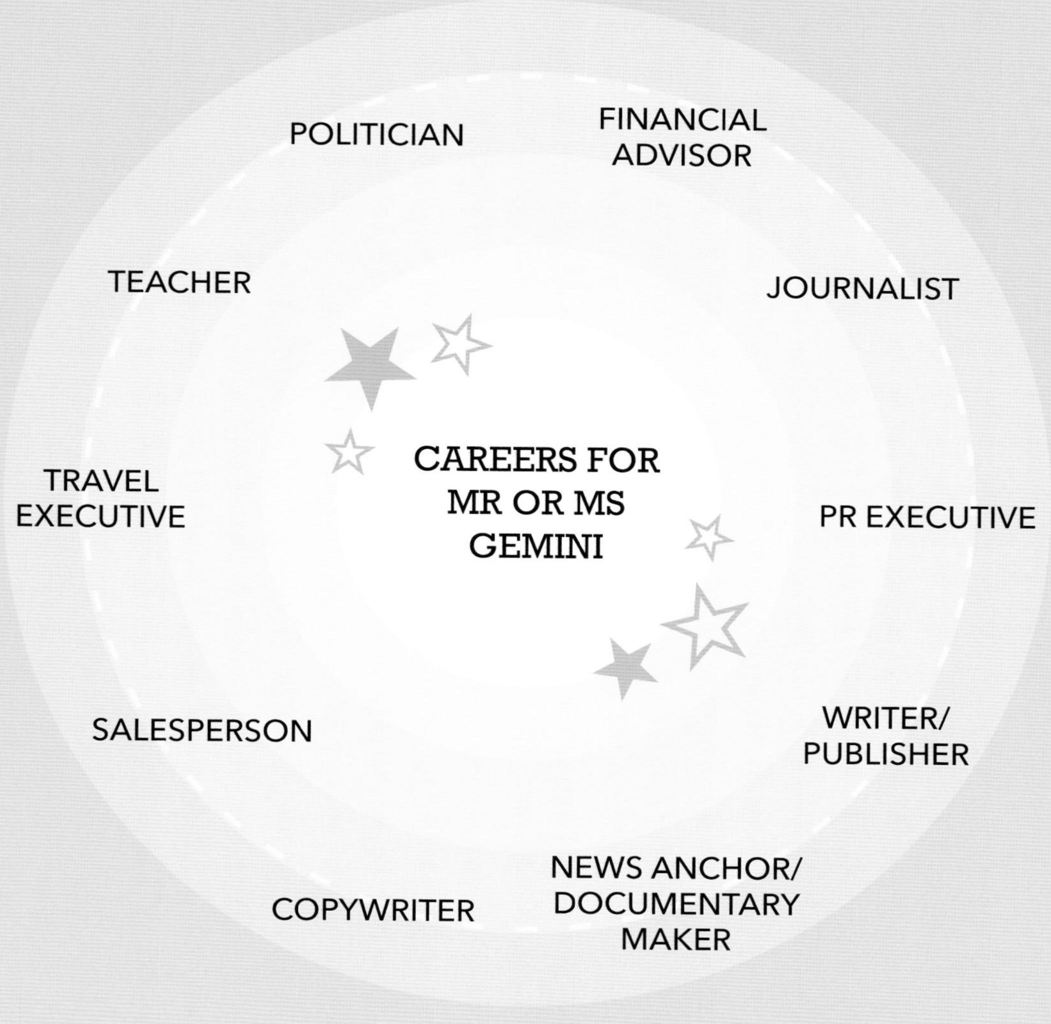

POLITICIAN

FINANCIAL ADVISOR

TEACHER

JOURNALIST

TRAVEL EXECUTIVE

CAREERS FOR MR OR MS GEMINI

PR EXECUTIVE

SALESPERSON

WRITER/ PUBLISHER

COPYWRITER

NEWS ANCHOR/ DOCUMENTARY MAKER

LIBRA IN THE WORKPLACE

22 SEPTEMBER–22 OCTOBER

Element: Air
Modality: Cardinal
Ruling planet: Venus

CURRICULUM VITAE

Libra comes in on or around 22 September, just as the season of mists and mellow fruitfulness begins, and, in tandem, there is a softness and grace, even an opaqueness about this sign that separates it from the other two air signs, Gemini and Aquarius.

In large part this is due to Libra's ruler, Venus – the planet of love and all things nice. Librans are people-pleasers and relationship experts, yet they can be sybarites and over-concerned about the appearance of things – not just their own image but the way situations are presented, which sometimes means rather a lot is swept under the carpet. And, of course, Librans can be terminally indecisive and indefinite.

Actually, it is not that Librans are indecisive: they usually know exactly what they want, but they dither because they wouldn't want to offend anyone or be seen in a bad light.

Librans always want to look good.

In their CV Librans would include the ability to

> **STRENGTHS**
> Unbiased
> Considerate
> Diplomatic
> Great negotiating
> skills
>
> **WEAKNESSES**
> Indefinite
> Two-faced
> Manipulative
> Procrastinating

mediate between warring factions, to negotiate a way through an impasse, to create a harmonious atmosphere in the workspace and to keep conflict and controversy at bay. Their skill set would make them eligible for careers in law, the judiciary, counselling, the arts, fashion and design.

They are the beautiful people.

The scales which symbolize Libra are there for good reason. Libra weighs everything in the balance and aims to give a fair and impartial judgement in all circumstances. However, in its efforts to be unbiased and never to come down hard on one side or the other, this sign can appear weak and vacillating. Which it is not.

Libra belongs to the Cardinal[12] family and the Cardinals are high achievers and self-motivators. In Libra's case, while it may look as though butter wouldn't melt in his (or her) mouth and that ambition is a dirty word, in his graceful way, often through deft social engineering, he gets to the very top of whichever pile he's aiming for.

The constellation Libra lies next to Virgo – indeed part of Virgo strays into Libra's

12   The Cardinal signs are Aries, Cancer, Libra and Capricorn. See the section on *How Astrology Works*.

territory – and there's a mythical connection between the two: Virgo's symbol, the Virgin holding the ear of corn, is none other than Astraea, the virgin goddess of justice. Which is a roundabout way of introducing the curious phenomenon that some of the properties associated with Virgo belong to Libra, and vice versa.

Take perfectionism for instance. This is a Libran quality, not a Virgoan one. Virgos are painstaking and driven to deliver always of their best, but perfectionism is about being perfect. And for Libra this is not just being the best you can be, but the best ever.

They are the perfect people.

THE LIBRAN BOSS

Close your eyes, take a deep breath and smell the roses. You're in the company of Chief Libra. And there may well be fresh-cut roses on the desk and certainly a pleasant aroma circulating around the office. These Venus-ruled bosses believe that even if business can get dirty that doesn't mean your surroundings should be shabby.

Regardless of how classically handsome or beautiful Librans may be, they will exude an aura of attractiveness. You will want to be in their company and do their company proud. In their presence you will feel you are the most valued member of the team, and if you had concerns before you entered the inner sanctum, they will be completely wiped away by the time you leave.

So far so good. The trouble is what Libra says and what ultimately transpires can be rather different. Putting you at your ease, putting out fires, are Libra's stock in trade, but in the space between leading you to believe one thing and the eventual outcome he or she will be figuring out how to do the exact opposite without upsetting you and looking bad to everyone else.

Indeed, it can take a very long time for the Libran boss to reach a decision, whether it be where to hold the annual do or how to expand the business. Weighing up the pros and cons and examining the situation from all angles may seem a worthy practice but it can infuriate those with whom Libra does business as well as members of staff. Occasionally, the boat of opportunity has left port by the time Libra makes up his or her mind.

Ideally, Mr and Ms Libra need a period of quiet meditation before passing judgement. And they should not be rushed. Pile the pressure on a Libran chief and any decision is almost guaranteed to be reversed in the days that follow.

Libran bosses are partial to taking a poll before making an important move. They will seek opinions from the office cleaner, their partners and their assistants – even the pizza-delivery guy could be called upon to cast his verdict. They all go into the Libran pot to be distilled into a semi-coherent plan. Clearly, there has to be some room to manoeuvre should things change...

Libra cannot thrive in an inhospitable or inharmonious environment. To this end, the Libra boss will do everything to create a pleasing physical space for his staff to work in – tasteful and stylish artwork may grace the walls (and the pictures had better be hanging straight) as well as ingeniously placed plants and *objets d'art*, and cleanliness is mandatory. Don't even think of eating a hot, greasy hamburger over

your laptop: the lingering smell will do nothing for your image, and you'll be in 'bad odour' with the boss for a long time to come. Your offence could prove terminal.

In an effort to ensure harmony between members of staff, the Libran boss's door will always be open to those who have issues. Libra likes little better than settling disputes. Each side will be heard out; each case examined, and without rancour or bias, and eventually a compromise will be reached. Sometimes the dispute is settled simply because those concerned are sick and tired of having to go over the issues time and time again. They just want to go home.

Librans could be accused of being over-fond of the sound of their own voices.

While Libran bosses are diplomatic, courteous and considerate, don't for a moment think this means they are immune to fierce arguments. They may never actually lose their tempers, but they will badger and bait, counter and contest until they have proved their point or beaten you down. If you have a difference of opinion with your Libran boss, go into battle with a white feather in your pocket.

All Libras love to be loved, and the Libran boss is no exception. They'll go out of their way to talk to the lowliest member of the company and treat him or her like a valued colleague. And from time to time, loving your colleagues and employees can morph into falling in love with them. However, susceptible as Librans are to romance, they do not like getting their hands dirty, and although they may not be as commitment-phobic as Gemini or as terrified of intimacy as Aquarius, they rarely allow their heads to rule their hearts. Office romances seldom become happy-ever-after stories, and it's usually the object of their initial adoration that sustains the broken heart.

So, the first rule of company Libra is: don't assume his or her attentions are a prelude to deep and abiding love.

This aside, there's very little to complain about when it comes to your Libran boss. These are some of the easiest people to get along with: they're always going to hear you out, always going to appreciate where you're coming from and only too delighted to meet you halfway. You're going to love working under them.

THE LIBRA EMPLOYEE

In Libras' case, appearances are not deceptive. How they present themselves at interview is a true reflection of who they are. The time and trouble they have taken with their appearance mirrors the efforts they will make to meet the demands of the job. They have an excellent work ethic: their aim is to exceed expectations.

I could not find a scientific study that statistically proved Librans are the candidates most likely to succeed, but even if you decide not to employ Mr or Ms Libra, you will have been impressed by her (or him), and you may want to keep her details on file.

Not only do Libran employees give of their best, but they are charming, helpful and cooperative in the workplace. They hate atmospheres and will do everything in their power to defuse hostilities. They find it well-nigh impossible to turn down a request and if you need anyone to work overtime or win over a client, get Mr and Ms Libra on the job.

Despite their easy-going demeanour, however, these are ambitious people. Capricorn may make no secret of his aspirations; Scorpios, Leos and Arians may turn into street fighters to achieve their ends, but Libra makes the journey to the top look seamless. Yes, they will work hard and, yes, they will fine-hone their talents, but Librans understand better than anyone that success is not just about what you know but who you know.

Librans can turn networking and social-climbing into an art form.

Their social skills, their charm and their instinct for saying the right thing at the right time make them naturals for the PR industry. They are excellent event managers, wedding planners, agents and go-betweens. And, in keeping with the scales of justice, Librans are drawn to careers that involve mediation – law, especially divorce law, human rights and gender equality (equality generally) – and they make consummate politicians and ambassadors.

Members of team Libra are not interested in average. They want the best out of life. And to achieve the lifestyle they aspire to they will take on a second job or study to acquire extra skills. They are not motivated by money: money is simply a means to a certain standard of living. To get the best out of your Libran employees, give them responsibilities above their station and invite them

to sit in on top-level meetings or at least introduce them to people of importance. The more Librans feel admired, the better they'll perform.

Feed their ambition, not their sweet teeth.

Do not run away with the idea that Librans are superheroes, however: they have their weaknesses. One of the problems with always presenting a cool, calm and benevolent face to the world is that they bottle up emotions and anxieties. And Librans do not tolerate stress well. They require plenty of rest, and periods of intense effort must be balanced by periods of relaxation. Without such a balance, Librans' health will be compromised, necessitating occasional absences from work, typically due to migraines and other stress-related disorders.

Librans are also sensitive to smell. Bad odours can literally make them sick. Keep your Libran employee happy by never allowing fug to develop and placing odour-eating plants, like palms, in the workspace. Never ever put a Libra in a windowless room with strip lighting or seat him (or her) close to the lavatories.

Another potential negative with a Libran employee is his or her love life. Relationships are a cause célèbre for Libra, and when things go wrong, these individuals cannot entirely distance themselves from their misery, leading to mistakes and an uncharacteristically short temper. And a similar trend for carelessness occurs when they are newly enthralled. As for in-house romances, Librans are a magnet for office foxes, and since the path of true lust never runs smooth, you could find yourself dealing with some unwelcome resignations.

Given that Librans are the peacemakers of the zodiac, you may be surprised how aggressive they can be when protecting what is precious to them. Whether they're defending human rights, protesting unacceptable conditions or their salary, you can expect a long drawn-out battle until they have won you over. They are the champions of the workforce when it comes to the unfair and the insupportable. So, if your Libra employee comes to you with a request for a pay rise, save yourself the war of attrition and hand over the cash.

If you're looking for someone who will bring a little extra something to the workplace, a little *je ne sais quoi*, please hire a Libran. These individuals are not only as sharp as tacks, but an invaluable source of counsel and consolation. And they have such style. You'll look forward to coming to work.

HUMAN
RESOURCES
PROFESSIONAL

LAWYER

COUNSELLOR

DIPLOMAT

MUSICIAN OR
DANCER

CAREERS FOR
MR OR MS
LIBRA

AMBASSADOR

FLORIST

EVENT
PLANNER

INTERIOR,
FASHION,
OR SCENIC
DESIGNER

BEAUTY
THERAPIST

AQUARIUS IN THE WORKPLACE

19 JANUARY–18 FEBRUARY

Element: Air
Modality: Fixed
Ruling planets: Uranus and Saturn

CURRICULUM VITAE

Aquarius is a confusing sign. And the confusion begins with its very symbol: the Water Bearer. Surely Aquarius is a water sign? No, it's not. The water pouring from the urn borne by the 'water bearer' is ether, the mysterious substance once thought to suffuse the realm of the gods. Aquarius is the third and last of the air signs, and the most complex.

Aquarius belongs to the Fixed[13] modality. Imagine for a moment air, which by its very nature is limitless, locked in an underground tunnel. Air, the thinking function, which should have free rein, is now constrained and forced into a narrow channel. On the plus side, this 'Fixity' enables the conceptual power of Aquarius to acquire focus and for Water Bearers to be firm in their opinions and intentions, yet this same function lends a certain rigidity and austerity to the sign.

> **STRENGTHS**
> Unsnobbish
> Independent
> Inventive
> Inquiring
>
> **WEAKNESSES**
> Resistant
> Contrary
> Controlling
> Detached

13   The Fixed signs are Taurus, Leo, Scorpio and Aquarius. See the section on *How Astrology Works.*

Another reason for this sign's complexity is its dual rulership. Before the discovery of Uranus in 1781, Aquarius was ruled by Saturn. Saturn is associated with boundaries, rules and regulations, law and order, facts and figures, terms and conditions. Uranus, however, is an altogether different entity – quite the rebel. In keeping with its eccentric orbit, Uranus brings a quirky, unpredictable and highly individual quality to Aquarius. Some Water Bearers resonate more strongly with Saturn while others respond to the call of Uranus, yet from time to time the 'inferior' ruler will present itself, making all Aquarians to some extent idiosyncratic.

Aquarians are a law unto themselves.

Aquarius comes in as winter's frigid grip tightens on the earth. The days are short; the nights long. Nature is busy underground, animals are in hibernation and humanity hunkers down. In tandem, Aquarius conserves its resources; it does not scatter its energies; it looks to the future.

Aquarians are the humanitarians of this world, the guardians of the future and the people prepared to boldly go where no man has gone before.

Their astro CV equips them for careers in the aerospace industry, travel, especially flight, and science, as well as the futures business, astrology included. Indeed, the astrologers' degree is 28 of Aquarius. And as an extra piece of trivia for you – that degree is exactly opposite the fixed star, Regulus, the ruler of Leo, Aquarius' opposite number.

In keeping with its Fixed nature, Aquarians tend to be the specialists of the zodiac. They are the experts, the talking heads, the pundits, the know-it-alls. They focus their minds on specific tasks and, unlike Gemini and Libra who will change and adapt their course as they go, Aquarius sticks to the plan. And this is crucial to understanding Aquarius; regardless how open-minded they may appear, they follow their own star. Relentlessly.

They are always true to themselves.

THE AQUARIUS BOSS

You have arrived on time for your interview. You are seated, waiting in reception while the meeter and greeter you have attempted unsuccessfully to engage in conversation is clacking away on an impressive-looking computer. After ten minutes of silence, your confidence fading along with your hopes, you will be set even further on the back foot when the person you believed to be the receptionist turns out to be the boss. Now, it may be that your Aquarian chief was fielding an emergency which meant there was no time for proper introductions, but it is just as likely to be a test.

Aquarius likes to play with your mind.

Now, thoroughly discombobulated, you are ready to get to know this unpredictable, engaging and every so often rather scary boss. At least if you're dealing with the Uranian variety. These individuals resist any kind of pigeonholing and resent conforming to the expectations of their lofty role. The Uranian prefers the casual approach to almost everything: he or she will be dressed for comfort and will want to be referred to by his or her first name, better still a nickname. Uranian bosses do not have staff but friends who happen to work for them. He or she may be there when you arrive early for work or appear at four in the afternoon. The door to the office will always be open and there will be a constant stream of people through it. Forget about set lunch breaks or getting home on time. Mr or Ms Uranus goes with the moment, which sometimes involves going without food and missing the last train home. What you will gain, however, is a sense of being part of an amazing journey.

In this type of Aquarian's world, revolutionary ideas will be born that will make the company a market leader. You will be thrilled and proud to be part of an extraordinary team. Things may get a little hairy at times – the Uranian boss isn't good at signing off on tax returns and paying the utility bills on time, and occasionally your salary will be late – but you will lie, cheat and steal for this boss. All right, that's an exaggeration, but the Uranians command great loyalty from their staff, not only for their genius but their disarming charm and endearingly awkward attempts at revealing their humanity.

The Saturnine Aquarian is an entirely different cup of tea. He (or she) will share some of the traits of their next-door neighbours, the Capricorns. This boss will run a tight ship. Staff meetings will be regular, pay checks will arrive on the correct day, and your salary will increase along with the rate of inflation. You will be expected to toe the company line at all times, dress and behave appropriately and to accept your place in the scheme of

things. There may not be any fireworks, but your job will be safe, and in the event that the company runs into difficulties, you will be given plenty of notice, and a reference, based on an accurate account of your performance, will follow.

The Aquarian who resonates with Saturn will feel a parental responsibility toward his or her staff. You can come to this boss with problems of a personal nature, and you will get a fair hearing. You won't be mollycoddled but won't feel dissed either. This boss will enquire after your family and be open to meeting and mingling with them. And, like a parent, you will be expected to look up to him or her.

And speaking of looking up to your Aquarian boss. Despite the spirit of brotherhood oft attributed to this sign, it produces more than its share of divas and dictators, a trend more usually associated with its opposite sign, Leo. However, in keeping with all polarities, the seeds of autocracy can sprout just as easily in Aquarius. If you have an Aquarian tyrant for a boss, you probably won't last very long. This individual hires and fires like a piston, and the office resembles a seething hub of tension and fear.

Inasmuch as both types of Aquarians can become autocrats, both tend to spring changes on members of staff and business partners. Again, this is partly a by-product of their personality and partly a strategy. They can agree terms, shake hands and then half an hour later pull out of the deal. In many instances

this behaviour has the effect of confusing and weakening the other party, which puts Aquarius in the position of being able to strike an even better deal in the aftermath.

The Aquarius boss is super smart, and well-schooled in the art of brinkmanship.

Water Bearer chiefs want to be your friend, but don't get too close. All the air signs require a degree of personal space, but Aquarius needs twice as much. Get too touchy-feely with them and you'll feel an arctic wind bearing down on you. And it goes without saying that developing an attraction for your Aquarian boss is a complete no-no. The Aquarian office is not a breeding ground for romance, love or sex, and certainly not happy-ever-after stories with the top dog.

As you must have gathered, Aquarian bosses are in a league of their own. You either love them or hate them. If you intend to work for one you'll need to be sure of yourself, fearless, thick-skinned and ready to accept praise and insults in equal measure. And the reward? A journey you'll want never to end.

THE AQUARIUS EMPLOYEE

Aquarians are neither leaders nor followers. They are individuals, but not loners. They enjoy company and working as a team. All right, that's their old PR machine kicking in: in reality Aquarians can be very awkward to work with since they have a unique take on things, and with their Fixed natures they can dig their heels in and become remarkably high-handed when others do not share their opinion. Fortunately, since Aquarians have ideas light years ahead of most people they are a positive boon to any company aiming to become a market leader. When the Aquarius employee has an idea, people listen.

As I explained in the section on the Aquarian boss, there are two types of Water Bearers: those who resonate with Saturn and those with Uranus. The former will be able to tolerate a nine-to-five existence, although at some point (probably around the age of 42 and the Uranus opposition) they will throw up their safe and secure job in order to follow their dream of being their own boss or becoming the screenwriter they always wanted to be. The Uranian will struggle with routine and is far better suited to self-employment or working for organizations which allow for flexitime.

Yet whichever Aquarian you have working for you, a degree of independence will ensure you get the best out of him or her.

Aquarius is the sign of science and technology, which is why so many Aquarians find their niche in these industries. And even if they opt for a career in academia or hospitality or the Civil Service, they embrace new technology with élan and are the first to have the new iPhone or some such gadget. If you have an employee who is a tad nerdy, a bit of an oddball, he or she will almost certainly have Aquarius in the chart. And if you think this makes the Water Bearer uncharismatic, think of Lisbeth Salander (*The Girl with the Dragon Tattoo*) or Indiana Jones who tick all the Aquarius boxes.

Your Aquarius employee has intelligence and intuition. He or she need not have gone to university, but it is a sign that likes to have letters after its name and credentials from an esteemed body. To this end many Aquarian employees will study in their own time to acquire qualifications or simply to slake their thirst for knowledge. When you employ an Aquarian, you're getting a first-class mind.

Water Bearers are the fount of all knowledge in the workplace.

And in keeping with their high-minded natures, Aquarians would opt for a poorly paid but prestigious position rather than a highly paid job offering little or no kudos. The Water Bearer is not mercenary and cannot be tempted to sacrifice his or her principles on the altar of Mammon.

Aquarians are never yes-men. They are not afraid to buck the trend or to argue against the prevailing wisdom. They can, of course, hold some extremely unorthodox opinions, but out of ten ideas, nine of which will never gain traction, one will turn out to be sheer genius.

Your Aquarius employee is likely to have a rebellious streak. It may not emerge in the early days of employment but, at some point, something will strike the Water Bearer as unreasonable or non-PC or against human rights and, unless he or she can be accommodated, your Aquarian will walk. These are some of the most altruistic and idealistic folk in the zodiac. And you will be wasting your time trying to impress Water Bearers with your status or, worse, pull rank on them – you will be treated with silent indifference.

Aquarians do not take well to authority.

They do, however, like to be the authorities on this and that. And if you want your Aquarian employees to perform to the max, feed their intellectual egos. They are your to-go place for knowledge and consultation.

Aquarius is the sign of brotherhood, and its members set great store by their friendships. They may love working for you, but don't get between them and their comrades. They will prioritize events with friends and drop everything, even that uber-important assignment, to go to their aid. If you employ an Aquarian, you'll be taking on a team. And they can be addicted to social media. Yet in any workplace you'll probably find opinion divided as to who likes Mr and Ms Aquarius and who does not. And strangely enough, the Aquarian is often completely oblivious to the fact that someone does not like him.

As employees, Water Bearers take a little work, but once you've understood how to work with them, once you have accepted their little quirks and shown respect for their wisdom, hardly a day will go by when you won't have some reason to thank providence you employed them. They're like having a little wizard in the workplace, ready to rustle up a little bit of magic just when you need it.

TECHNICAL
WRITER/
SPEECHWRITER

POLITICAL
ANALYST

LAB
TECHNICIAN

ACTIVIST

CAREERS FOR
MR OR MS
AQUARIUS

ELECTRICIAN

AEROSPACE
ENGINEER

ANYTHING TO DO
WITH THE TECH
INDUSTRY/ARTIFICIAL
INTELLIGENCE

ASTRONAUT

HUMAN
RIGHTS
SPECIALIST

AIR-TRAFFIC
CONTROLLER

INTER-RELATIONSHIPS
Who gets on with whom in the workplace

AIR-AIR

Same element combinations have their virtues and their vices. On the one hand, air signs in the workplace will always put projects before passion, so any differences of opinion between them only pique their creativity: they can't be doing with frosty silences – life is too short; let's move on. The air–air workplace is immensely

sociable, stimulating and fun. On the other hand, air signs can rate style over substance, so as they cheer each other on, exploring ever more amazing possibilities, the germ of an idea becomes lost and the realization of the project ever more remote.

A workplace with a preponderance of air signs tends to be all talk and no action.

Clearly, it depends upon the mix of air signs in the workplace. Gemini and Libra can get along with pretty well anybody, so there will be harmony even if not all projects come together in time – or ever. And with a strong Gemini-Libra workforce you may want one or two earth signs to make sure those castles are built with bricks and mortar, not air. Water Bearers with their Saturn/Uranus rulership are more grounded and can bring their ideas into reality, but they're not always easy to work with, even amid a strong air team.

Indeed, Aquarius as the exception to the air rule is a recurrent theme. While Geminis and Librans place a high emphasis on socializing with colleagues both in and out of the office, Aquarians prefer to separate their work lives from their personal lives. And they like their own space. While Gemini and Libra will be happy to toss ideas back and forth endlessly – Libra, in particular, loves to share – Aquarius likes to focus on specifics and form a solid structure.

Airy people are ideas people and best suited to careers which use their creative imaginations and their intellectual skills. All businesses need air signs in order to move with the times – and beyond them – but you probably wouldn't want too much air in the caring professions or industries that do not require or encourage freedom of thought – the Civil Service, for instance.

AIR–FIRE

Fire warms air while air fans the flames. A workplace with a good mix of fire signs and air signs is a company made in heaven. This is an ideal combination.

Fiery Aries, Leo and Sagittarius and airy Gemini, Libra and Aquarius are positive and outgoing signs. They have little time for angst and cannot exist in an environment where there are back-biting and low ceilings – the latter literally and metaphorically. They rub along well together and bring out each other's best qualities.

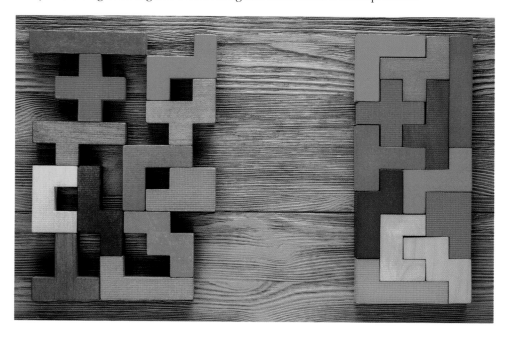

Here you have the combined power of rational thought (air) and intuitive action (fire).

Air can analyse the probable outcomes of fire's ambitions without squashing its enthusiasm while fire can encourage airy people to get their ideas off the ground without giving them too much time to change their minds.

The benefit of a team nicely balanced between air and fire is that there is little conflict. Yes, there may be stimulating arguments and occasional rank disagreements but nothing to frighten the horses. They meet their problems with the intention of finding solutions – and find them they will.

If there is a downside to a fire/air group, it is that sometimes they get carried away with the glorious potential of a project and fail to dot the Is and cross the Ts. And, as we all know, the devil's in the detail.

Some fire and air combinations work better than others; the reason being one of the air signs will be a fire sign's opposite number. Put another way, an Aries-Libra combination, a Leo-Aquarius mix and a Sagittarius-Gemini team belong on opposite sides of the zodiac, and opposites both attract and repel. So, although you still have the winning combination of fire and air, there can be a little extra tension between opposite signs.

A workplace strong on air and fire is suited to businesses that involve ideas and action: news organizations, magazines, advertising companies, head-hunting establishments and travel and transportation.

AIR-EARTH

Air may play an essential role in transporting the seeds that make earth fruitful, but winds and breezes stir up plenty of dust. Consequently, earth/air combinations can be fractious in the workplace, although not half as awkward as in romantic and sexual relationships.

The earth signs find Gemini, Libra and Aquarius a tad lightweight and far too charming for their own good. They may even describe them as empty shells. Air signs, on the other hand, tend to feel stifled by earth's slow and conservative manner. They sometimes refer to them as troglodytes. Fortunately, neither element group allows emotion to overcome reason, so while a hard frost may descend on boardroom meetings from time to time, they'll usually find consensus, even if it is only to agree to disagree.

One of the reasons that earth and air make sense in the workplace is that they are ruled by the same planets: Saturn rules both Capricorn and Aquarius; Venus rules both Taurus and Libra and Mercury rules both Virgo and Gemini. And a shared rulership makes for an innate understanding of and respect for each other's standpoint. Capricorn and Aquarius understand the need for structure; Taurus and Libra share a need for harmony and form while Virgo and Gemini are natural disseminators – to both, knowledge and information is the very stuff of life.

Where an earth sign shares a modality with an air sign, there is a common bond, so Capricorn and Libra, Taurus and Aquarius and Virgo and Gemini represent the best of the air/earth combinations, although when this working relationship goes sour it can become irreversible. Someone has to go.

Earth, as we know, is intensely practical; air is theoretical, but in business this can work. Those earthy seeds that air can disperse mean that some of earth's brilliant ideas that might otherwise never get off the ground actually find a home.

Another plus to their mutual disregard for emotions in business is that finances do not scare them. Money is money; it's a commodity. In investment houses and merchant banks across the globe air and earth signs keep a cool head and a firm grasp on the tiller when markets collapse and currencies are devalued.

Despite their very different natures, there is some fertile common ground between air and earth signs. They may even be the best of the combinations in the workplace.

AIR-WATER

Think of a breeze wafting over a lake. See that gentle ripple? Then imagine a hurricane striking a body of water... As in nature, so with the elements air and water. These are essentially antithetical energies. While air is at home in the realm of the mind and experiences great discomfort in the world of feelings, water belongs to the realm of emotions and has difficulty living in a rational world.

Air is detached from its feelings; water is consumed by them.

In an office space, air and water signs should keep a safe distance from each other. In principle both have

much to offer one other but, in reality, the two just don't belong in the same room. Gemini, Libra and Aquarius are continually frustrated by the water signs' need to check how they feel about something before they can move on it. They become exasperated by the water signs' mood swings and their tendency to take everything personally. If only they had a degree of detachment, all would be well...

For their part, Cancer, Scorpio and Pisces feel the air signs lack depth, patience and emotional intelligence. They see them as cold and lacking in compassion and empathy. In response the water signs shut down and play passive-aggressive games. Admittedly, Libra can relate to another person's sensibilities and do a good job of demonstrating empathy, but even Librans can only stomach so much mollycoddling. As for Gemini and Aquarius: are they bothered? No.

In the early days of an air/water relationship – both in the workplace and the bedroom – there will be a deep fascination between the two. Air will be drawn to the mystery of the water signs, their ambiguity and inconsistencies, while Cancer, Scorpio and Pisces will be impressed by the air signs' brilliance and eloquence.

Of all the air/water combinations, those that belong to the same modality are the most difficult yet have the most potential to achieve great things: Gemini and Pisces, Libra and Cancer, Aquarius and Scorpio.

As always, how well these two elements get on in the workplace depends on other factors in their charts. An air sign with, say, the Moon in Cancer, Scorpio or Pisces, will have an affinity with a water sign that can allow an extremely good working relationship to develop and, vice versa, a water sign with the Moon in Gemini, Libra or Aquarius will find common ground with an air sign. Air signs bring coherence to water's concepts and water signs bring depth, meaning and texture to air's theories.

But without such chart connections, air and water are always going to have a bumpy ride.

STAR RATING BETWEEN GEMINI, LIBRA AND AQUARIUS AND THE REST OF THE ZODIAC

	GEMINI	LIBRA	AQUARIUS
ARIES	★ ★ ★ ★ ★	★ ★ ★ ★	★ ★ ★ ★ ★
TAURUS	★	★ ★ ★	★ ★
GEMINI	★ ★ ★	★ ★ ★ ★	★ ★ ★ ★
CANCER	★	★	★
LEO	★ ★ ★ ★ ★	★ ★ ★ ★ ★	★ ★ ★ ★
VIRGO	★ ★ ★	★	★ ★
LIBRA	★ ★ ★ ★	★ ★ ★ ★	★ ★ ★ ★
SCORPIO	★	★	★ ★
SAGITTARIUS	★ ★ ★ ★	★ ★ ★ ★ ★	★ ★ ★ ★ ★
CAPRICORN	★ ★	★ ★ ★	★ ★ ★
AQUARIUS	★ ★ ★ ★	★ ★ ★ ★	★ ★ ★ ★
PISCES	★ ★	★	★

THE
WATER SIGNS
CANCER, SCORPIO
AND PISCES

THE ELEMENT WATER

Almost all metaphysical and psychological systems include a four-fold division: the four temperaments, the four humours, Jung's four functions... even modern physics divides matter into four fundamental states (although other states are known to exist). And in the same way that no one temperament, humour, function or state is better than another, no astrological element is superior to another. Of course, water is essential for life...

The oceans cover 71 per cent of the Earth's surface and contain 97 per cent of the planet's water. Without water nothing would grow, and Earth's surface would blister and crack. The element water is thus associated with fertility; it is synonymous with nurture.

Water has no shape of its own, no substance: it needs to be contained. To this end, Cancer, Scorpio and Pisces require others to give form to their hopes, dreams and visions. They function better when they have support and guidance, which is why they work particularly well with the earth signs who they believe they can trust and rely on. The water signs do not appreciate being shaken and stirred by the more outgoing and dominating fire and air signs.

Cancer, Scorpio and Pisces are secretive, they have their deeps and they feel safe there.

In Jungian psychology, the Feeling Function correlates to the element water. Cancer, Scorpio and Pisces belong to the realm of feelings; they are subjective and reactive. And although it might follow that the water signs are therefore passive and introverted, this is simply not true: you've only got to consider the power of water, whether in the form of a tidal wave or a hydro-electric plant, to comprehend that water signs are a force to be reckoned with.

Each of the water signs ends a four-fold series: Cancer concludes the first quarter of the zodiac – Aries (fire), Taurus (earth) and Gemini (air); Scorpio concludes the second – Leo (fire), Virgo (earth) and Libra (air); and Pisces completes the third and final quadrant – Sagittarius (fire,) Capricorn (earth) and Aquarius (water) and, indeed, the whole zodiac. In this way the water signs bring together all dimensions of experience as depicted by the different elements in preparation for the next cycle to begin.

The water signs are multi-layered; they're never Johnny-one-notes. Think you've got a grip on a water sign and Cancer, Scorpio or Pisces will slip through your grasp, disappear into vapour or turn into ice. They require careful handling and need considerable understanding. However, they are a vital part of the workforce. These individuals are caring, compassionate, visionary and selfless, which is why you'll find so many of them in the healing and helping professions, the arts, the spiritual industry and hospitality. In the workplace, if you need someone to provide

tea and sympathy, band aids and painkillers and liberal amounts of ginger biscuits, locate a water sign.

Cancer, Scorpio and Pisces mend broken bones and broken hearts.

The water signs are in touch with their feelings, they understand nuances and see aspects of situations hidden to others. Since feelings are by their very nature unconscious, Cancer, Scorpio and Pisces do not always know what drives them and quite how things will turn out – they feel their way forward. Sometimes this feeling approach to life in general, and work in particular, generates confusion and uncertainty but mostly their insights and intuitions prove invaluable.

Each water sign is different, however, due to its modality[14]. Water in its purest form, so to speak, is Pisces. Pisces is a Mutable sign and therefore dispersive and equivocal; water's fluid nature is even more uncontainable in Pisces. Cancer, on the other hand, is Cardinal – a modality that is self-driving and achievement-oriented – while Scorpio is Fixed, rendering this water sign tough and uncompromising.

Each water sign is different also because of its ruling planet. While Cancer is ruled by the inconstant moon and is quite the moodiest of the water signs, Pisces is ruled by Neptune, the most elusive and mysterious of the planets. As for Scorpio, its ruler, Pluto, has dominion over the underworld, and is synonymous with the process of transformation – death and rebirth.

Oceans, seas, lakes, ponds, streams, rivers and estuaries are all made up of water. On a calm, sunny day, the waterways are pleasant to be on or near; they promote relaxation, respite and reflection, but on a stormy night these same waters become dark and dangerous. And so it is with the water signs. Most of the

---

14   There are three modalities: Cardinal, Fixed and Mutable. See the section on *How Astrology Works.*

time they are wonderful to be with; they listen to you, comfort you, and are your bridge over troubled waters, yet on a bad day these nurturers and protectors can devastate you.

At some point all water signs turn on someone they have loved or admired: Cancerians do it with a sideways snipe, Scorpios with a poisoned 'dart' and Pisceans by disappearing without explanation, never to be found.

Both Cancer and Scorpio have aspirations. They may not show their ambition, but in the way of water continuing to beat against the shore and thus eroding the land, they persist, they are patient, they wear down the competition and eventually their time comes. Pisces' ambitions rarely lie in the world of work: they are attuned to worlds you cannot see, they care little about material rewards and the spoils of power and fame.

There are degrees of wateriness, though, and whether you are an Aswan Dam of insights, feelings and yearnings or a sprinkler system delivering adequate amounts of emotion and intuition depends on how many planets and points you have in air signs besides the Sun in your birth chart.

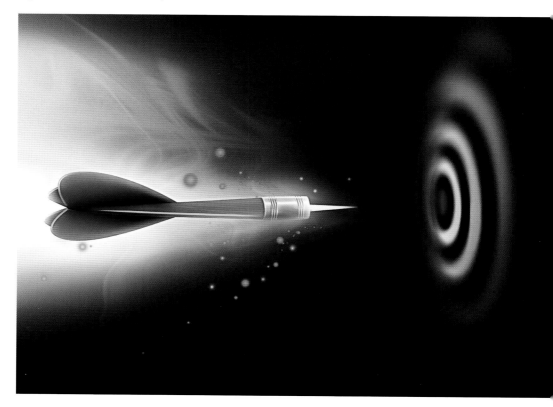

WATER ON A SCALE OF 1-10

If you are curious to know just how watery you or your boss, colleague or employee are, you'll need a birth date and, ideally, also a time and place of birth. Whether you use an online service to tabulate the chart for you or you yourself have the knowledge, establishing the degree of sensitivity is easy: add up all the planets and points in water signs, according to the list below. It's simply a numbers game.

Ascendant = 3	Venus = 3	Saturn = 2
Sun = 3	Mars = 3	Uranus = 1
Moon = 3	Mid-heaven = 1	Neptune = 1
Mercury = 3	Jupiter = 2	Pluto = 1

If you score 9 points or more in water signs, you are awash with sensitivity; between 5 and 8 your feelings lead the way, but not all the way all of the time; and between 1 and 4 you have just enough empathy and emotional intelligence to get by.

Elizabeth Taylor: 13 points in water.

People with a surfeit of water experience great difficulty in distancing themselves from their emotions. You cannot always reason with them, and you cannot always be sure how they will react to a similar set of circumstances on any given day.

They can take you on a magical mystery tour or dump you at the bottom of the ocean.

The late Elizabeth Taylor (Pisces) had a surfeit of water. With a total of 13 points in water signs, she was mesmerizing on screen and in real life; her battle with her weight and her eight marriages reflect the inconstancy and inconsistency of too much water. Princess Diana (Cancer) may only have scored seven points on the water scale, but her compassion and empathy, her magnetism and her vulnerability also make her an ambassador for the water element.

Sometimes a surfeit of water in a chart inspires a love of the sea and all things related to the world of water: David Attenborough (a tally of ten points in water, and a rising Mars in Pisces to boot) and undersea explorer and inventor of the aqualung, Jacques Cousteau (six points in water, and a Mars-Neptune conjunction in Cancer) are cases in point.

Bill Gates (Scorpio), business magnate, humanitarian and author, epitomizes the generosity and philanthropy of super-watery people – a total of ten planets and points in water signs – while Pablo Picasso (Scorpio and a sum of nine points in water signs) demonstrates the artistry and visionary genius of the element.

Indeed, many great painters are strong in water – Claude Monet, Marc Chagall, Rubens and Degas – as are many illustrious writers, including Marcel Proust, Ernest Hemingway, Franz Kafka and George Orwell. And there are a glut of actors, dancers and musicians with planets and points in water signs – Frédéric Chopin, George Frideric Handel, Tom Hanks, Meryl Streep, Katy Perry, Carlos Santana, Rudolf Nureyev and Sylvie Guillem.

Bill Gates: 10 points in water.

For balance, however, I should add the roll of dishonour: Leona Helmsley (Cancer), the 'Queen of Mean', cult leader Charles Manson (Scorpio), and Adolph Eichmann (Pisces), who is said to have masterminded the Holocaust.

CANCER IN THE WORKPLACE

22 JUNE–20 JULY

Element: Water
Modality: Cardinal
Ruling planet: Moon

CURRICULUM VITAE

The first thing we need to know about the sign of Cancer is that it is ruled by the Moon, the one celestial object we can see on a daily basis, provided, of course, you don't live in a cloudy country like England. And just in case you've forgotten, the Moon is not a planet but a satellite, although that has no bearing on its value and interpretation in astrological terms.

The Moon in astrology represents the great feminine principle. The 28-day menstrual cycle mirrors the Moon's journey through the zodiac, and pregnancy and birth and motherhood are ruled by the Moon.

'O swear not by the moon, the inconstant moon that monthly changes in her circle orb, lest that thy love prove likewise variable.' Juliet's plea to Romeo has some astrological truth to it. While the Moon's cycle from new to full and back again indeed reflects the changeable nature of Cancer, this sign of all the water signs craves constancy, stability and security.

STRENGTHS
Kind
Persistent
Compassionate
Dedicated

WEAKNESSES
Passive-aggressive
Negative
Manipulative
Crabby

The sign of Cancer begins as the sun reaches its highest point in the sky at the summer solstice or, to be more technical, when the sun, in its apparent journey along the ecliptic, reaches its northernmost point. In ancient times, this midsummer moment was celebrated in style: bonfires would be lit, maypoles danced around – all such rituals aimed at inspiring and celebrating fertility.

Which yet again underscores Cancer's powerfully progenitive properties. Cancerians like to grow things from scratch and nurture them through to full bloom – and then some.

Cancerians find it terribly difficult to let go.

Cancer is no exception to the water-sign rule: still waters run deep. Their gentle, diffident personas mask dogged ambition. Like all members of the Cardinal family, they are highly motivated, but their great advantage is their perseverance and persistence.

The celestial Crab's CV is unlikely to list many and varied career choices. Crabs set out with a target in mind, and once they've found their desired job, they'll stay until the organization folds. If you want someone to run your company through good times and bad and to nurture it through crises and conquests alike, choose a Cancerian; and if you need an employee who will take a personal pride in nursing any and every task he or she is given, take on a Cancerian.

You will find members of this water sign in all industries – they can be celebrated entrepreneurs (Richard Branson), brilliant artists, musicians and writers (Meryl Streep, Oscar Hammerstein III and Jean-Paul Sartre) and award-winning doctors and scientists (Professor Robert Winston and Elisabeth Kübler Ross) but they are especially suited to careers in the healing professions, therapy, childcare and security.

Cancerians need to be needed.

Meryl Streep: Sun and Venus in Cancer.

THE CANCER BOSS

Richard Branson is an outstanding example of the Cancer boss. No shrinking violet he, yet despite his dashing appearance and derring-do he is a caring, conscientious and compassionate man. Your Cancer boss, once he has taken you on, will look after you, be there for you through your dark days and ensure you have a pension to cover your needs when you are long gone from the company. He may continue to send Christmas cards even when he himself has retired.

But like all people who appear calm in all weathers, beneath that composed exterior a cauldron of emotions will be bubbling. The Cancer boss is extremely sensitive: the smallest remark can be taken out of context, analysed and deemed to be a sign of imminent rejection. You won't know, of course: he or she will still be smiling and conducting business, but after a while you'll get a funny feeling that something indefinable has gone wrong.

When under a perceived threat, the celestial Crab disappears into its shell and won't come out until he or she feels safe and has figured out a way to deal with the situation. The offender may be forgiven (the slight, never forgotten) but it is entirely possible he or she will be temporarily or permanently frozen out.

Richard Branson: Sun and Uranus in Cancer.

All Cancerian bosses have the power to turn water into ice.

Learn to recognize your Cancer boss's moods and adapt accordingly. When he or she has gone into silent mode, leave well alone and only enter the inner sanctum bearing favourite snacks and beverages, and speaking in a soft voice.

Cancer is a proud sign; Crabs cannot bear to lose face. Failure is not an option. To this end they play the avoidance game. They side-step awkward situations, leave the building when people on the 'frozen' list are expected and will never be seen performing a task that could in any way make them look silly. (Please don't take this boss on a karaoke night.) If you want to be the employee of the year, every year, recognize what fazes your Cancer boss and cover for him or her.

The Cancerian boss is a home bunny. Crabs love their creature comforts and being in the bosom of their family. So much so that the office will have a homey feel to it. Home comforts may include soft furnishings, photographs of family and pets and a fully functioning kitchen or at least a spot where food can be stored

and prepared. Cancerians are comfort-eaters: food is the common denominator whether celebrating or commiserating. And if you want to win this boss's affection, bring home-made goodies to work on a regular basis.

The love of family also extends to the business. Employees are treated as family and complete loyalty to the company is expected.

The Cancer CEO will give precedence to the family of members of staff who apply for a job, and if the boss moves to a new company he or she will take as many of the team as possible. You'll never have a problem asking this boss for time out because your child care provider let you down, your six-year-old has a temperature of 101 degrees or your mother lost her cat or her mind.

Money, money, money. Now, the Cancerian boss likes to make money not because he or she is avaricious but for the security it provides. However, hand in hand with making money goes thrift, which just occasionally turns into extreme miserliness. The Cancer CEO will keep a close eye on company finances and should you ask for a rise, you may be surprised at the frost that descends on the meeting. Gentle persuasion, perhaps with a pluck at the heart strings, is more likely to get you a salary increase.

The Cancerian boss drives a hard bargain.

Other less laudable traits about this boss include Cancer's tendency to be manipulative and passive-aggressive. Very few Cancerians tell it as it is: they require time to examine all angles of a situation; they rarely, if ever, reveal their true opinions, feelings or plans. Crabs in nature are not aggressors, but they can deliver a lot of pain when stepped upon. Do not underestimate these kindly, cuddly bosses. Remember, they have pincers.

In keeping with their Cardinal modality, Cancerians make good leaders and decision-makers: they may take their time reaching a conclusion, but once they've made it they follow it through until it is completed. They also care about their employees and associates – they would rather put themselves at risk in a dangerous situation than one of their team. They are tenacious, strong-willed, courageous and tactical; they care.

They may even be the best bosses in the zodiac.

THE CANCER EMPLOYEE

 The Cancer employee is not looking for excitement, challenge and diversity; he or she is seeking a job that will last for life, or at least until retirement, and provide a generous pension and healthcare to boot. What these very private individuals will not reveal at their job interview is their desire to work with superiors and colleagues they can trust, superiors and colleagues who never put fame, glory and a fat salary before the people they care about.

Cancerians need to know they are in a safe place.

Do not expect Mr (or Ms) Cancer to tell you much about his personal life. He will have a list of interests and hobbies, which he's happy to talk about; he'll discuss his past employment, his education, his favourite books/places/foods but he'll shut up like a clam when probed about his personal life. It's really none of your business.

Celestial Crabs make good managers. They are good with people and excellent at pinpointing strengths and weaknesses and therefore adept at putting the right person in the right place. Cancerians find a natural home for their abilities and interests in the food, health and hospitality industries and in human resources. They like what they do to be useful and geared to making people healthier, happier and more comfortable.

Cancerian employees do not rate professional and financial success above their home and personal life. However, they are not without ambition. All the Cardinal signs have aspirations, and Cancerians are particularly hard-working and tenacious. They may not talk openly about their desire for high office, but by stealth and patience they will get there.

Also, although they may want assurances, they'll be working in a safe place – both in the sense of the security of the premises and the people who inhabit it – they aren't easily deflected from their ambitions, and will meet a challenge and the competition with courage and a very clever strategy.

All celestial Crabs know how to circumnavigate the object of their desires. A practice mirrored by their occasional sideways gait.

Your Cancerian employee will take instructions well, she (or he) will carry out orders to the letter, and no matter how ill she may feel or how many obstacles she has to surmount, the job will be done. The only exception to this rule – and it's a big exception – is the advent of a family dilemma. As a boss, you'll have to swallow your indignation at being let down by your otherwise single-minded and dedicated employee because it is

the youngest's first day at school: someone else will have to ring the opening bell at the NYSE (New York Stock Exchange).

Some people want money because it buys power and beautiful things; Cancerians want money because of the security it provides. These celestial crustaceans worry dreadfully about the future; they fear an impoverished old age and the inability to provide for their loved ones. Negotiating a salary, a raise or any kind of financial deal in which they have a personal interest is conducted with a quiet but ferocious tenacity of purpose. You must either lose the argument or your valued Cancerian employee.

Thus far it seems that employing a Cancerian is a plus-plus situation. But there are minuses. Celestial Crabs have a vengeful streak. If you hurt them, they will pay you back, no matter how long it takes. You will have long forgotten the crime you committed against them when you feel their outrage. So, do not take for granted their kindness, their hard work and selfless devotion. The payback will be painful.

In keeping with the hard shell that protects the crab's soft and vulnerable interior, all Cancerians put on a tremendous front. Do not be fooled. This employee will not take well to being reprimanded or criticized in front of others, nor will he

or she appreciate being the butt of a joke. Treat this employee with solicitude and you'll be singing his (or her) praises for the term of his employment. Humiliate him, disrespect him and at the very least he'll be on your conscience for years.

Cancerians never forget where they buried the hatchet.

If you remember only one thing about your Cancerian employees, it is that they crave affection. They simply cannot function in a hostile environment. Show them your approval, shower them with affection (don't get too close, of course) and they will perform at the top of their game. They have very little ego involved in their desire to please and succeed: it is all about being valued and cared about.

Remember this and you'll bless the day your Cancerian employee entered your office world.

HOSPITALITY
WORKER

ANTIQUES
DEALER

CHILDCARE
WORKER

HOME
ECONOMICS
PROFESSIONAL

MIDWIFE/
GYNAECOLOGIST/
OBSTETRICIAN

CAREERS FOR
MR OR MS
CANCER

HISTORIAN/
ARCHIVIST/
CURATOR

GENETICIST/
GENEALOGIST

NOVELIST

BAKER/CHEF/
CATERER

BREAST
ONCOLOGIST

SCORPIO IN THE WORKPLACE

23 OCTOBER–21 NOVEMBER

Element: Water
Modality: Fixed
Ruling planets: Pluto and Mars

CURRICULUM VITAE

The sign of Scorpio comes in as autumn peaks. The trees are bare and the fallen leaves have all but vanished back into the ground. The warmth of summer is long gone, replaced by frosts and storms. The days are short, the nights long. Halloween is upon us. As befits a sign ruled by Pluto, lord of the underworld, it is the season of death and decay and things that go bump in the night.

It matters not, by the way, that Pluto is no longer considered a planet. Whether it is a planetoid or a celestial dwarf, astrologers have been monitoring its effect since its discovery in 1930, and its principles of death and rebirth and transformation have not changed. Pluto is the most mysterious of the planets: its small size belies its density. It packs a powerful punch... as do all Scorpios.

Before the discovery of Pluto, Mars was said to rule this sign, and although Scorpio resonates with the combative and courageous properties of Mars,

STRENGTHS
Committed
Persistent
Passionate
Loyal

WEAKNESSES
Vindictive
Secretive
Jealous
Inflexible

its depth and darkness and its extremist nature has much more in common with its modern ruler.

The observation that still waters run deep is true for all water signs but in Scorpio's case you're in the hadal zone – the deepest of the deep, named for Hades, the Greek god of the underworld. And incidentally, one of this mythical figure's attributes was the ability to make himself invisible.

Then there is the symbol for the sign – the Scorpion. A nasty little creature that might just kill you and can certainly cause you a lot of pain; a crustacean that can withstand extremes of temperature – you can even put a scorpion in the freezer and it will survive – and isn't afraid to attack an enemy, regardless of its size.

Goldie Hawn: Sun in Scorpio.

All these things tell you a lot about Scorpio people. They are as tough as titanium, they'll survive any amount of flak fired at them. It's do or die; all or nothing.

Regardless of their fearsome reputation Scorpios have their loveable side. Admittedly it is attached to a steel backbone and conceals their stockpile of WMD's (Words of Mass Destruction) but there are plenty of notable and much-loved individuals who belong to Pluto's team, as well as some less lovable characters. Goldie Hawn, for instance, and Leonardo DiCaprio, Ryan Gosling, Hillary Clinton, Gordon Ramsey – oh, and Marie (let-them-eat-cake) Antoinette.

Scorpios bring commitment, passion and drama into the workplace. They are best suited to careers that involve research, stealth and endurance. If you need someone to get to the bottom of anything, advertise for a Scorpio.

THE SCORPIO BOSS

 You may have been warned before you met your Scorpio boss for the first time that his bite was worse than his bark, but what you may not realize is that Mr and Ms Scorpio admire courage and love a challenge. Come across as a submissive, sugary sap and you'll never make the grade. Stand up to them, prove you're made of the right stuff, and you'll be in their employ until you're ready to draw your pension, or until you betray their trust. Which, if you're wise, will never ever happen.

Like all water-sign bosses, the front they present to you bears no relationship to what they're actually thinking. A charming, friendly discussion can belie their intention to fire you, while a hard-nosed exchange could be a precursor to a promotion. At the best of times Pluto's people are difficult to read but when they have a specific end in mind, they'll lead you right up the garden path.

Scorpios love to deceive. Their hobby is weaving webs for the purposes of entrapment.

This boss will endeavour to get to know everything about you. Your deepest, darkest secrets are not safe. The Scorpio chief can spot a disconnect in a heartbeat and will dig and dig until he or she gets to the truth. It is pointless leaving something out of your personal or professional information. This boss's radar will seek out the 'oversight' and it will inspire further in-depth research.

Needless to say, the Scorpio boss wants you to know very little about him or her.

Privacy and secrecy are second nature to the Pluto CEO. To this end drawers and cupboards will have locks and important documents stuffed into fake cans of peanuts. There could be hidden cameras, to all intents and purposes for security, but they serve a secondary function in watching staff. And since these bosses are capable of going to such extreme lengths to establish what is going on in their office world, they are completely paranoid about anyone doing the same to them.

No water sign has quite the same capacity as Scorpio to turn water into ice. And it is a phenomenon to watch out for. The quieter a Scorpio boss gets, the more potentially dangerous the situation becomes. When a stream of vitriol has turned to ice it's time to leave the building. Possibly forever and without your belongings.

Now, if all this makes you think there are no redeeming features to working for a Scorpio chief, you'd be wrong. These individuals know what they want, and they'll get it, come hell or high water. They are never average. They nurture big ambitions, and they have the temperament and the tenacity to fulfil them. They like to be in the top league of whatever industry they are in, and they have an excellent instinct for choosing the right people to get them there. And if you're working for a Scorpio employer, that means you. You can be proud of yourself.

Scorpio bosses can also have kind hearts. They won't want to appear sentimental, but they will come to your rescue if you justify their help, and they will often do so in a behind-the-scenes way. Even their good deeds are conducted in the shadows. Prove to your Pluto employer that you are loyal and committed to the cause, and you'll always be given a hearing, and a leg up.

Of course, there is a fine line between gaining your boss's sympathy and inspiring scorn. Scorpios despise weakness in others almost as much as they despise it in themselves. And you don't want to bring out the bully in them. It's not nice.

Change: Scorpios do not like change. They may be courageous, but they don't like change. If a strategy or a saucepan has served them well for 25 years, why get rid of it? So, one of your jobs is to get Mr or Ms Scorpio to move with the times. Challenge is your best tool. 'I hear Joe Smith has brought in a whole new system that will revolutionize sales of his product. Obviously, we wouldn't be interested in doing anything like that. I mean, who puts profit over tradition? If he wants to be a market leader, then let him...'

Competition is a great spur to the Scorpio boss. Even if it requires bulldozing an ancient model – or even the entire premises – it will be done.

Finally, we come to jealousy and possessiveness. The Scorpio boss isn't just over-protective of the people he or she loves, but the circle of trust encompasses anyone who works for or has dealings with the company. You may believe it is only good practice to fraternize with senior members of the organization or even the competition, but such behaviour will be interpreted as incipient disloyalty. And you know what happens when water freezes.

So, treat your Scorpio boss with respect, but never toady up to him (or her). And never fail to look him in the eye. Respect goes two ways in Pluto country.

THE SCORPIO EMPLOYEE

 Scorpio employees don't do middle-of-the-road. When they're good, they're fabulous, and when they're bad, they can destroy your business. All right, that's an exaggeration, but these are the extremists of the zodiac and until they've worked for you for a while you won't know which end of the spectrum you've got, and even then, given enough provocation, the most dedicated Plutonian can turn rogue. It's best you keep a close eye on them, but only as long you don't let them catch you doing so.

Scorpio employees don't take well to being scrutinized – that's their job.

Right from the off, you need to know you're dealing with an individual who isn't easily intimidated. The clue lies in that *Mona Lisa* smile, that direct, unflinching gaze. There's something about their presence that makes you ever so slightly insecure and on edge. Is there a trace of toothpaste on your lips? Could he or she have overheard that awkward call? What is the reason for that deep sigh?

And even when your Scorpio employee has worked for you for years, you may still wonder what's really going on behind that enigmatic persona. Like all good poker players these employees have studied you and observed your tells; they can read you like a proverbial book. And by the same token they know how to conceal their intentions. (Remember, one of Pluto's super-powers was invisibility.)

If you're going to have a hope of successfully handling your Plutonian, you must understand Scorpio's relationship with power. All Scorpios desire power. On the one hand, these ambitious arthropods can have their sights set on fame and glory and the top job, and on the other, they just enjoy being able to manipulate situations because of what they know or who they know. Like the Cancerians and the Capricorns of this

world, Scorpios do not mind how long it takes them to reach the pinnacle of their ambitions; and in some ways the harder it is the more driven they become.

Offer your Scorpio employees the opportunity to advance, push them to extremes, and they'll more than measure up. They'll be a credit to you. And you'll be indebted to them. Underrate them and continue to pass them over for promotion, and the least of your worries will be that they leave.

Scorpios believe in retribution. They also know revenge is a dish best served cold.

Intense drive and determination are the hallmarks of this Pluto-ruled sign. You can be sure your Scorpio employee will not let you nor the team down, even in the face of dire adversity... at least as long as you have commanded their loyalty. Betray their trust and they'll delight in taking you down: they'll be the first people to march to tribunal in the event of a dispute.

The paradox is that although members of this sign crave power and are not cowed by those in power, they're not brimming with self-confidence. Like all water signs, Scorpios are ridden by angst; they spy ulterior motives and hidden messages in the most innocent of gestures; they believe certain

people have it 'in for them' or are deeply envious of them. So they are almost permanently under extreme tension. And should that tension build and prove unbearable, a Scorpio employee will sabotage a perfectly good situation.

Scorpios can be very difficult to understand.

When Pluto's people self-destruct, despite appearances to the contrary, it serves a useful purpose. Since members of this sign do not embrace change, periodic acts of self-destruction do the job of change for them. Transformation is a process innate to Scorpios; like a phoenix, they rise anew out of the ashes of denouements they have brought upon themselves. No one is as capable of reinvention as a Scorpio. Which is why so many of them have two or three totally different careers during a lifetime.

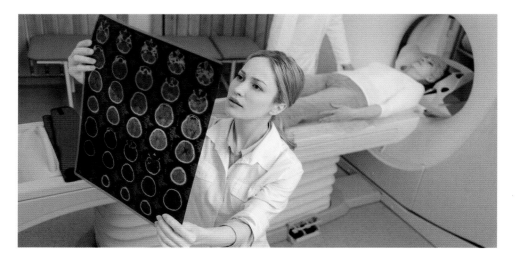

Scorpios do well in jobs that allow them to dig and delve. They have excellent powers of analysis and are extremely focused. Psychology, psychiatry, espionage, criminology, forensics and bacteriology – these are Scorpio things. And even if they've had to settle for a mundane job, they'll make themselves indispensable with their ability to dig up the unknown, the hidden and the potentially lethal. Even those Scorpios that make their way into the arts and the creative world will be drawn to the darker aspects of existence; they will draw deeply on their emotional, physical and intellectual reserves.

So, you have one or more Scorpios in your employ. You're going to love them or hate them. They're going to be your salvation or your scourge. But every office should have one. They are not only the only people who can get to the root of any anomaly, but they are shrewd, single-minded, resourceful, resilient and capable of doing all the unpleasant jobs no one else would do. Oh, and one last recommendation: they have a wicked sense of humour.

SPY

PSYCHOLOGIST/
PSYCHIATRIST/
THERAPIST

PROFILER

CRYPTOGRAPHER

CAREERS FOR
MR OR MS
SCORPIO

ONCOLOGIST/
UROLOGIST

CRIMINOLOGIST

RESTORATION
TECHNICIAN

RADIOLOGIST

FUNERAL
DIRECTOR

INVESTIGATOR

PISCES IN THE WORKPLACE

19 FEBRUARY–20 MARCH

Element: Water
Modality: Mutable
Ruling planets: Neptune and Jupiter

CURRICULUM VITAE

In Cancer we find the water of rockpools and the seashore, in Scorpio that of the fjords and glaciers and in Pisces we meet the ocean. This water sign has little in common with babbling brooks and still ponds: like Earth's great seas, at one moment calm and cobalt blue and the next grey and storm-tossed, Pisces' moods and mores are inconsistent and unpredictable; they can be gentle and supportive or turbulent and treacherous.

The sign of Pisces not only concludes a fourfold element group but closes and completes the entire zodiac. It is as if the whole of the zodiac experience is absorbed and coalesced in Pisces. Which is why it is often referred to as the dustbin of the zodiac.

This third and final water sign comes in as winter draws its last breath and goes out as spring announces its arrival. It is thus a sign that encapsulates the notion of circularity – 'In my end

STRENGTHS
Adaptable
Non-judgemental
Self-sacrificing
Instinctive

WEAKNESSES
Addiction-prone
Escapist
Disposed to martyrdom
Woolly-minded

is my beginning.' And there is both a melancholy and joyous innocence about the sign.

We understand much about Pisces from its ruler, Neptune, the god of the underwater world, and companion to Greek Poseidon, the deity of oceans and earthquakes. Neptune in astrology is the bringer of dreams; its nature is fluid and deceptive. In Neptune we find heaven and connect with our soul; yet this same planet can plunge us to the bottom of the ocean through betrayal and perfidy.

Neptune was discovered in 1846, just as the great romantic and spiritualism movements were sweeping the globe. And in keeping with such things, Pisceans are the great romantics of the zodiac and the most spiritually driven. Before the discovery of Neptune, Jupiter was allotted rulership of Pisces, and it is courtesy of this planet that Pisces gets both its tendency toward excess and its generosity of spirit.

Pisceans are at once the most loveable people on the planet and the most baffling.

As befits a sign that resonates with the mystical and the divine, Pisceans run the gamut from saints to sinners and high achievers to absolute losers; it is a sign that produces geniuses and crackpots and those whom the gods love and those whom the gods torment. Consider for a moment these names from the Pisces hall of fame: Albert Einstein, Liza Minnelli, Justin Bieber, George Washington, Rihanna and Steve Jobs.

Pisceans can fit into any job you care to name, but they are particularly drawn to the arts, the healing and helping professions and those careers that require imagination, humanity and creativity.

THE PISCES BOSS

Pisces and power rarely belong in the same sentence. These are not people who seek high office; it comes to them. Take George Washington for instance. After driving the British out of America, he chose not to anoint himself king but gave the American people the right to shape their own destiny. He displayed the innate selflessness of Pisces. He put the people before power and glory.

Piscean bosses will not have got their top job by treading on the broken bones of their competitors or schmoozing those who matter; they will have got there because they followed their instincts, remained true to their vision and were unattached to outcomes.

The typical Pisces boss is not concerned with appearances; he (or she) is concerned with meanings. He wants to know the whys before the hows. Like the method actor who must know what maketh the man before he can claim the character, the Piscean has to own his vision before he can bring it into reality.

Regardless of whether Mr or Ms Pisces is running a merchant bank, a publishing company or a film studio,

Liza Minelli: Sun in Pisces.

he or she will bring imagination and innovation to the job. It is Pisceans' extraordinary leaps of faith and clarity of vision that propels them into the spotlight and turns their companies into national and international names.

Sitting in the boardroom with your Piscean boss, however, you may wonder why he is not remonstrating with the culprit who got the figures wrong and caused the company to lose out on a major opportunity. (We'll come to issues with correction and discipline shortly.) Instead, he appears to be gazing out of the window at a flock of Canada geese. He's not really looking at the birds: he's wondering whether they're a sign of something, and maybe, just maybe, a joint enterprise with Grey Goose vodka might be in order.

George Washington: Sun and Venus in Pisces.

Pisceans are prone to checking out of difficult conversations.

This Fishy boss is, however, a good listener. He or she will give your ideas, your opinions, your complaints and your worries a good hearing. And since Pisces is the sign of helping and healing, your boss will feel bounden to save you from harm and ease your pain. The only trouble is, sometimes his or her good intentions get lost and forgotten in a sea of other projects, possibilities and the occasional personal dilemma.

Also, just occasionally, the Pisces boss's attentions will be misinterpreted, and many a divorce or marriage is the result of a little too much misplaced caring and sharing on behalf of the Fishy CEO.

One of the reasons Mr and Ms Pisces are so sympathetic to their staff's problems is that they have been there themselves. They know what it's like to fail, to be

rejected, to sail too close to the wind, to have loved and lost, and they identify with your suffering.

Which brings us to the aforementioned issue of 'difficult conversations'. The Piscean boss is not cut out to chide and discipline, let alone give you notice. In an attempt to soften bad news Mr or Ms Pisces will coat it with so much sugar syrup that the employee in the firing line may end up with a raise and a key to the executive gym.

What all Piscean bosses need is a hatchet man: a bad cop to their good cop, a Peter Mandelson to their Tony Blair. That way, the company ship keeps a-sailing and staff numbers remain at a manageable level. And if you work for a Piscean boss, you yourself might end up taking on that mantle of responsibility.

Given that the Piscean boss is strong on imagination and creativity, he or she often has a shortfall in practicality. Likewise, making money is not a primary goal. Spending it, maybe... In consequence, this boss should never be allowed to handle company admin, let alone taxes and health and safety requirements. The irony is that the Piscean employee is often very good at book-keeping and administration.

In Pisces office world there is a place for everyone.

At the risk of repeating myself, Pisceans are not comfortable with the trappings of power and position – they'd rather every day was dress-down Friday – and this is the least likely sign of the zodiac to head a large corporation. This having been said, if that corporation were the BBC or the National Theatre, Mr and Ms Pisces would be in their element. (No pun intended.) Their natural habitats are the arts, hospitals, parks and recreation, welfare, charities and those worlds that require freedom, movement and creative expression.

While some other zodiac bosses make a song and dance about top-notch food and dining facilities, the Piscean boss sees virtue in a fully stocked bar, or at least a couple of good bottles of wine. He or she understands how much smoother a negotiation can be when accompanied by liberal amounts of alcohol. And if you want to show your Fishy boss your admiration, bring him or her a rare single malt or an estate-bottled Pinot Noir.

Working for a Piscean boss has many pluses: no day will be quite the same as another; you don't need to explain yourself – he or she is completely in tune with you – and just when you despair that order will never come out of the chaos, something totally magical happens. And if you're lucky, you'll find that under his or her guidance you too will get to work in the land of make-believe and be paid for it.

THE PISCES EMPLOYEE

If your new recruit arrives a little late on the first day of work, proffering a tale of the unusual and the unexpected and a box of assorted doughnuts, there's more than a chance you have a Piscean in your employ. Random events are an occupational hazard for the celestial Fish – they are to the weird and the wonderful what bees are to honey.

The Pisces employee will bring something a little different, even a little mystical, to the workplace. He or she may have excellent organizational skills and a flair for figures; it matters not, they'll still bring an element of the fantastical to work with them. However, these individuals are more suited to jobs where their imagination can run riot and where they believe they are serving a greater purpose. They're happier in unstructured environments and in organizations where they are given free rein to express themselves and their talents.

From here on in, however, your grasp on the Piscean employee is going to get increasingly slippery.

One statement will be followed by another that completely contradicts the first. But, you see, this is Pisces on a plate – a mass of contradictions; fascinating but paradoxical.

For the most part your Piscean member of staff will be helpful and supportive, cheerful and kind. Pisceans have an uncanny sixth sense which deploys the moment they feel something is wrong or someone is in need. Mr (or Ms) Pisces knows instinctively what is required and has a knack of being in the right place at the right time and, according to him, even the wrong place and time invariably turns out to be right.

There's a reason for everything, as Pisceans are fond of saying.

Nevertheless, this staff member does not enjoy being the unpaid help. Pisceans love to be needed but after a while they begin to resent the casual way their kindness is taken for granted. But rather than put their foot down, Mr or Ms Pisces will become less and less available and more and more snappy. Eventually, they will hand in their notice.

Pisceans are rarely fired: they know when to leave.

Piscean employees are sensitive souls. They won't be able to give of their best in a workplace full of fire and air signs – people who are loud, assertive, smart and sassy. They need to be surrounded by equally gentle souls, preferably from the earth

element upon whose shoulders they can lean and who can defend them against attacks of the verbal and emotional kind. Given that Pisceans are on the fragile side, they are better off working on their own, so make sure you give Ms (or Mr) Fish an office to herself or at least a desk in a corner near the window. Better still, allow her to work from home.

Sometimes the innate Piscean vulnerability results in health issues. The Fish, especially when anxious and upset, can sprout an illness or an allergy, thus requiring time off and a lot of modifications to his or her workspace. (Pisceans have an instinctive aversion to technology; please don't force them to use the microwave.)

Pisceans can be otherworldly. They may choose to place crystals around their workspace and wear little amulets, and since they are particularly sensitive to bad energy, they might suggest the use of a smudge stick to cleanse their surroundings. This may be a bridge too far for some employers and colleagues, but the chances are that in Mr or Ms Pisces' hands, suddenly everything feels better and brighter.

Pisceans are not motivated by money. This does not mean they'll work for free, but it does imply they put job satisfaction above and beyond remuneration. So, if you want to get the best out of your Pisces employees, you'll need to praise and coddle them. They may not always be able to meet a deadline – Pisces' muse doesn't operate under the gun – but what eventually comes out of their labours and their creative imaginations will be more than worth the wait and the anxiety.

Can we talk romance? Pisceans tend to fall in love at the drop of a hat. You may not be able to control or protect their tender hearts out of office hours, but on work territory you need to keep them well away from the office flirt. As great romantics they believe in promises made in the heat of passion, and when betrayed and deceived there is no one more devastated – and unable to work. It really is in your best interests as an employer to stamp on a burgeoning office romance before

you end up having to replace your most talented member of the team. The Pisces, that is.

The Piscean employee is never going to fit into a straitjacket of your making, or anyone else's come to that. They're independent spirits, motivated by their feelings and instincts. They prefer to swim with the current but occasionally, and without notice, they'll head upstream to more fertile breeding grounds. Metaphors aside, you're not going to employ Mr or Ms Pisces because they'll conform to the norm; you need them for their unique take on life in general and your business in particular.

If any sign can take you to the stars, it's Pisces.

CHARITY
WORKER

COUNSELLOR/
ADDICTION
SPECIALIST

SOCIAL
WORKER

MEDICAL
PROFESSIONAL

CRUISE DIRECTOR

CAREERS FOR
MR OR MS
PISCES

PODIATRIST

MARINE SCIENTIST

FILMMAKER/
CINEMATOGRAPHER/
PHOTOGRAPHER

PSYCHIC
MEDIUM

SCREENWRITER

INTER-RELATIONSHIPS
Who gets on with whom
in the workplace

WATER-WATER

Water signs have a natural affinity for one another. They're coming from the same place. They feel on home territory – feel being the operative word. As long as there is consensus and communion, there is no better team than team water, but when storm clouds gather a water ship heads for the rocks, and it takes a devilishly long time to get it re-floated.

You can recognize a workplace with a preponderance of water signs: it will be very quiet; a haven of silent industry; each person will be working in their own space at their own pace. Occasionally someone will head to the refreshment zone, bringing back something for everyone – water signs always know who prefers what – which inspires a gentle murmur of approval. Sometimes, however, that pleasant quiet turns into an uncomfortable silence – someone got offended and no one wants to talk about it.

Cancer, Scorpio and Pisces are sensitive, creative, thoughtful, considerate, hard-working and a tad paranoid. Lots of water signs in a business team can support and inspire one another but they also feed each other's fears and insecurities, compromising production. And when one of them takes offence and emotionally shuts down, it can be very difficult to get the team back into balance and production. Likewise, if one water sign pours cold water on an idea, the others quickly lose confidence. Scorpio and Cancer have the power and tenacity to get people back on board but all too often they will have taken some kind of personal

stance on the issue and dug their pincers in.

Members of the same water sign bring out each other's best and worst qualities. On the one hand, Crabs become more creative and, on the other, more cranky; Scorpios kill it (in both senses) while Pisceans together can work miracles or go round in ever-decreasing circles.

Different water signs make a better mix and of all three combinations, Pisces with Cancer or Scorpio is best. Pisces has the capacity to drift away from conflict, so differences of opinion soon get resolved. Scorpio/ Cancer combos can mutually self-destruct; they're both ambitious and defensive and competition between them can be fierce. Also, both Crabs and Scorpions tend to hang on to the past, which means that even when an impasse between them is bridged, they never forget it. It comes back to haunt them.

The issue with a predominantly water workplace is that emotions drive everything. On a good day you couldn't find a happier and more effective bunch but on a bad day, you might as well shut up shop.

WATER-EARTH

Water nourishes earth, enabling it to become fruitful, while earth holds water and prevents it from running all over the place. Both the fire signs and the water signs bring creativity and inspiration into the workplace, but while Aries, Leo and Sagittarius run rampant over earth's need for structure, discipline and caution, Cancer, Scorpio and Pisces encourage the earth signs to go beyond the boundaries of their imagination. They bring out the best in them.

Earth's stability and dependability is a perfect foil for water's insecurity and vulnerability. The earth signs rarely feel hot and bothered as they do in fire's company, nor ruffled and confused as in air's vicinity. Water responds instinctively and undemandingly to earth while earth to them represents strength and steadfastness.

The exchange between earth and water signs is pleasant and rewarding. There's a nice little hum in the office. They like to sit near each other and hang out together at the coffee station. Cancer, Scorpio and Pisces are not the types to insist on their own way at all costs, although Scorpio can be bloody-minded at times, and they welcome

Capricorn's leadership, Taurus's commitment and Virgo's pragmatism.

The best earth/water combinations are those that involve signs that are 60 degrees apart: this is an angle of harmony and positive diversity. This is why Taurus's best workmates are Cancer and Pisces; Virgo's are Cancer and Scorpio and Capricorn's are Scorpio and Pisces.

Virgo is Pisces' opposite number in the zodiac and both belong to the Mutable family, so they share certain preferences, behaviours and each other's vices and virtues. Virgo and Pisces can go round and round in circles, sometimes losing the end game completely, and they both have passive-aggressive tendencies, but when they work well together, they're a brilliant team. They will, incidentally, be the supplier of pills and potions to the office population and the members of staff guaranteed to know the source of your sore thumb.

Capricorn is Cancer's polar opposite, and there is a mutual give and take to this working relationship. Taurus and Scorpio, by contrast, tend to bring out one another's worst points, although if there is one team guaranteed to go down with the ship it's going to be this one.

If there is a problem with an earth/water relationship it lies in their both being too cautious and pessimistic. While the earth signs maintain they're only being realistic, water signs cannot explain their reservations: they just feel something is not going to work, and they just know in their bones they're right. Thus, as a working couple they compound their mutual negativity, and this can slow down progress and ruin the normally warm and cooperative atmosphere.

But, by and large, earth signs and water signs make a great team.

WATER-FIRE

What happens when you pour water on fire? It goes out. And what happens when fire heats up water? It evaporates. Then again, steam heat is a force to be reckoned with. And where would we be without central heating? This is not an irredeemable combination, but it takes a lot of work.

In the same way that fire and earth are elemental mismatches, so are fire and water. While both fire signs and water signs are driven by their emotions and instincts, there is a tremendous difference in their basic temperaments. Fire signs are initiators; they don't need a lot of prodding and coaxing to bring their talents into the workplace; water signs, on the other hand, require nurture, encouragement and sensitive handling.

Aries, Leo and Sagittarius can be a tad too pushy and insensitive for Cancer, Scorpio and Pisces. When things go wrong, fire signs move onward and upward, working on the principle that eventually everyone will get over it and the next big thing will be the best big thing ever; water signs sulk and brood and silently plan payback. Thus, fiery folk are always shaken to the gills when the water sign they had considered no threat gets the promotion or rights a wrong for which the powers that be are forever in his or her debt.

Still waters run a little too deep for fire signs.

The way to get the best out of your water/fire team is to hold weekly in-house meetings to discuss issues and 'share'. (This might be irritating in the extreme for the fire signs, but it will work wonders for better office relations.) The sharing session should be held after an alcohol-free lunch. Fire gets animated on alcohol; water gets wistful.

Not all fire/water combinations are equal, however. Signs that are 90 degrees apart belong to the same modality, which tends to make for even more tension between them. Aries and Cancer, Leo and Scorpio and Sagittarius and Pisces have to work even harder on their relationship. Then again, the rewards are even greater.

WATER-AIR

Think of a breeze wafting over a lake. See that gentle ripple? Then imagine a hurricane striking a body of water... As in nature, so with the elements air and water.

These are essentially antithetical energies. While air is at home in the realm of the mind and experiences great discomfort in the world of feelings, water belongs to the realm of emotions and has difficulty living in a rational world.

Air is detached from its feelings; water is consumed by them.

In an office space, air and water signs should keep a safe distance from each other. In principle both have much to offer one other but, in reality, the two just don't belong in the same room. Gemini, Libra and Aquarius are continually frustrated by the water signs' need to check how they feel about something before they can move on it. They become exasperated by the

water signs' mood swings and their tendency to take everything personally. If only they had a degree of detachment, all would be well...

For their part, Cancer, Scorpio and Pisces feel the air signs lack depth, patience and emotional intelligence. They see them as cold and lacking in compassion and empathy. In response, the water signs shut down and play passive-aggressive games. Admittedly, Libra can relate to another person's sensibilities and do a good job of demonstrating empathy, but even Librans can only stomach so much mollycoddling. As for Gemini and Aquarius: are they bothered? No.

In the early days of an air/water relationship – both in the workplace and the bedroom – there will be a deep fascination between the two. Air will be drawn to the mystery of the water signs, their ambiguity and inconsistencies, while Cancer, Scorpio and Pisces will be impressed by the air signs' brilliance and eloquence.

Of all the air/water combinations those that belong to the same modality are the most difficult yet have the most potential to achieve great things: Gemini and Pisces, Libra and Cancer, Aquarius and Scorpio.

As always, how well these two elements get on in the workplace depends on other factors in their charts. An air sign with, say, the Moon in Cancer, Scorpio or Pisces, will have an affinity with a water sign that can allow an extremely good working relationship to develop and, vice versa, a water sign with the Moon in Gemini, Libra or Aquarius will find common ground with an air sign. Air signs bring coherence to water's concepts and water signs bring depth, meaning and texture to air's theories.

But without such chart connections, air and water are always going to have a bumpy ride.

STAR RATING BETWEEN CANCER, SCORPIO AND PISCES AND THE REST OF THE ZODIAC

	CANCER	SCORPIO	PISCES
ARIES	★	★ ★	★
TAURUS	★ ★ ★ ★ ★	★ ★	★ ★ ★ ★ ★
GEMINI	★	★	★ ★
CANCER	★ ★ ★	★ ★ ★	★ ★ ★
LEO	★	★	★
VIRGO	★ ★ ★ ★ ★	★ ★ ★ ★ ★	★ ★ ★
LIBRA	★	★	★
SCORPIO	★ ★ ★ ★	★ ★ ★	★ ★ ★ ★
SAGITTARIUS	★	★	★ ★
CAPRICORN	★ ★ ★ ★	★ ★ ★ ★ ★	★ ★ ★ ★ ★
AQUARIUS	★	★ ★	★
PISCES	★ ★ ★ ★	★ ★ ★ ★	★ ★ ★